Finger Strings

Finger Strings

A Book of Cat's-Cradles and String Figures

Michael Taylor

Stories and rhymes by Milly Reynolds and Jaimen McMillan

Floris Books

First published in 2008 by Floris Books, Edinburgh
Second printing 2012

© 2008 Michael Taylor

British Library CIP data available

ISBN 978-086315-665-6

Printed in Malaysia

Contents

Foreword

Many societies have developed a 'string-game' culture as a means of communicating their mythologies, passing time, social interaction and challenging their individual creativity.

Today, string games have found a new cultural identity as a crucial tool for the developing child; for those children for whom childhood can result in a lack of meaningful movement or opportunities to explore space, or who have fewer chances to interact with others and exercise their creative spirit.

As a learning-support teacher, I have witnessed the power of these string games; the pleasing coherence of the sequences, the element of surprise as the last step of the finger dance is completed and the unmitigated joy when the sequence works and the child stands above the creation and sees it in its entirety.

For the child who finds school an unrelenting struggle, these string games work to develop skills that can be transferred into motor agility, literacy and numeracy. The dyslexic child is supported to move from the tangible to the abstract, to learn fluid sequences through tactile and proprioceptive senses, which readies them for the world of written expression — the one they find so incomprehensible.

String games serve as an excellent mentor to the child learning to understand 'left and right,' 'up and down,' 'in front and behind.' Through these particular activities the child is given an opportunity to feel (and thus know more surely) the difference.

The fact that the creative work happens through the medium of the string allows errors to be easily redeemed. The child who, in the classroom, struggles to produce neatly-spaced and aligned written work can revel in the beauty achieved through the dance of their fingers. Corrections here do not appear as messy smudges but as perfected accomplishments.

In defining 'nimble' we arrive at 'easy to grasp.' By fostering fine motor dexterity and agility, we support 'ease of grasping' in other areas of development. The gleeful exclamation of 'I've got it!' when, for example, the 'Apache Door' stands before them, can become a fertile ground for other successes. Once a string game has been thoroughly learnt, the child can be challenged to 'try it behind your back!' or 'above your head.' The possibilities are truly endless, as are the fruits gained by awakening the human hand in this way.

Michael Taylor has, once again, brought these traditions alive and, through his own nimbleness, made them easily accessible for those who delight in creative playfulness and intelligent learning.

Ann Swain, Michael Hall Steiner School,
March 2008

Meet the String Man

There is a rich world-wide tradition of string games and, with a little imagination, a simple loop of string can turn into anything. It's magic; a magic that children can learn and experiment with to reflect the world they live in. Michael Taylor has witnessed how inspired children can be when shown how to make a few string figures. He has seen crazes develop after a demonstration in a class, in a scouts' meeting, at a party or in a summer camp.

As a teacher, Michael is absolutely convinced of how beneficial the learning of string games can be for a child's dexterity, co-ordination, creativity and imagination. He is presently teaching children with learning and behavioural difficulties and, in some cases, he has found string games can give a child a real sense of achievement and self-esteem, as well as encourage other social skills. A string can be a way to meet friends, entertain them, play tricks on them and share and learn with them.

String games can appeal to all ages. The oldest person who bought a string from Michael was ninety-five! His youngest enthusiasts, not yet five, happily make the stilts, the jumping fish and the magic flag and watch enthralled the walking caribou, the man climbing the tree and the lightning flash, much as they might watch a puppet show.

Michael likes to share his passion with others and always carries one string (or more) in his pocket wherever he goes. On tube trains, for example, he has seen one, two, then several people eager to join in and share what they knew when he started practising his ever-expanding repertoire. Some of the figures were new to him, others he knew by different names. He found that, apart from breaking the ice with strangers, string games kill time on long journeys and he thinks that every airline should have them in their travel packs!

Thanks to the International String Figures Association, cultures from Easter Island to Ghana, Siberia, Guyana, the Canadian Inuit, (yes, they are good for teaching geography too!) are now able to share each other's string game heritage. Most Europeans are familiar with 'Cat's-cradle' (a game for two), 'the barrier,' 'the cup and saucer,' 'cutting the hand' … Do any of these ring a bell? Ask your parents or grandparents. String games are a fantastic way to bridge the gap between generations. Some grandparents have forgotten how much joy could be derived from a simple loop of string in the pre-television era but in fact, the reintroduction of that simple activity can be a healthy way to balance out the external stimuli a 21st-century child is receiving.

Claudine R. Taylor
First published in *Pure Modern Lifestyle* magazine, August 2002

About String Games

World-wide Distribution

From Bhutan to Bolivia, Australia or Siberia, string games have been played for centuries. Some are special to their area, others — like 'Jacob's ladder' — are known almost everywhere and under many different names.

Cultural History

Occasionally, verses and songs accompany traditional string games. These can depict mythological characters. A story from the Assam/Burmese border tells of a popular tribal god who knows all the answers — including which string needs to be pulled! On Murray Island, Papua New Guinea, string figure songs are called 'Kamut Songs.' Some of the verses in this book continue these traditions.

Children's Game

'Cat's-Cradle' is often considered to be a children's game. 'The (Navajo) Drum' is known by almost every Navajo child and the 'Apache Door' is becoming known by children the world over as our cultures are shared.

Linking Generations and Crossing Languages

Adults too enjoy string games, sometimes to entertain the young, sometimes because of the intricacies and beauty of string art in itself, and sometimes as a way to study and record cultures from around the world. They have a special role linking generations and crossing language divides.

Types and Lengths of String

There is usually a local string appropriate for making string figures. Traditionally, children in Papua New Guinea used natural fibres; today they are taking colourful acrylic from the local bilum bag makers. The ends of nylon or polyester string can be melted under a candle flame, then squeezed together to make a loop. Cotton cord measuring 4mm (1/8 inch) in thickness can be knotted to make a loop. The usual length is 2 metres (6 feet), making a one metre loop, though some figures require a doubled (or shorter) string and some need a longer one.

Who is this Book for?

This book can be enjoyed by children and adults from five years to ninety-five years. Children will find many of the instructions easy to follow and adults will find source material for entertaining children or for their own interest. Early Years teachers and playleaders will find the chapters 'Simple Figures' and 'Stories' particularly useful in their work with the under-fives. Primary School Teachers and holiday playworkers will find many challenging 'Stars,' 'Moving Figures' and 'Tricks' to inspire and enthuse older children from seven to fourteen years. 'Partner Games' and 'String Things' can be introduced alongside stories and longer figures for variety. Teenagers can enjoy mastering figures like the 'Olympic Flag' (page 91), 'Running Caribou' (page 74), 'Frog' (page 67) and 'Thumb Jump' (page 110). Magic like the 'Indian Rope Trick' (page 115) and challenges like the 'Thrown Knot' (page 114) are included for those wishing to have a few party tricks up their sleeves. Instructions for making a 'Scoubidou String Man' (page 119) and a 'Whizzer' (page 123) are included for anyone wanting a craft-like activity. The book can be a starting point and introduction for hobbyists. Contacts and further reading are provided at the end for those who wish to continue to explore the fascinating world of string games.

Chapter Themes

The book is divided into string game themes: Simple Figures, Stars, Stories, 3D Figures, Popular Figures, Moving Figures, Other Figures, Partner Games, Tricks, String Things, Very Simple Figures, Children's Inventions and 'Stringing Stories Together.' The following notes on these themes will be of particular interest to teachers and performers.

1. Simple Figures

These simplest figures are ideal for teaching very young children (under five) or groups of older children (six to eight years old). Though many figures in this book can be made with most types of string, including strings made from wool, the 'Jumping Fish' (page 21) needs quite a stiff string and the 'Flag' (page 19) needs to be multi-coloured to show changing colours.

2. Stars

There are many traditional string figures of stars and constellations and some are not obviously connected to stars at first sight. The Navajo figure known as the 'Butterfly' (see page 66) is also the name of a Navajo star constellation. The 'Elastic Band Star' (page 28) and the 'Star in a Star' (page 30) were shown to me with elastic bands by two men from the Philippines on a train journey in England after they had claimed there were no string figures in their country! The 'Five Person Star' (page 32) has been made at numerous children's birthday parties. Sometimes the birthday child would enter the middle of the star after it

had been made while the others sang 'Twinkle, twinkle little star' and raised and lowered the figure accordingly.

3. Popular Figures

Popular figures include 'Fish spear' (page 46), 'Cup and Saucer' (page 36) and 'Jacob's Ladder' (page 38; also called 'Four Diamonds' and 'Indian Head-band') which have world-wide distribution. 'Apache Door' (page 40) is known by most Native Americans, although often by different names, and has been made popular all over the world ever since it was described in the first major book on this subject, written by Caroline Furness Jayne, *String Figures and how to make them,* which was published in 1906, as well as in many books since.

4. Stories

Some verses offered here continue the sing-song quality suggested by the 'Kamut Songs' (string figure songs) of Papua New Guinea. Party entertainers may find the 'Birthday Party' story (page 58) with its balloon, candle, accordion and party gift ideal for telling at birthday parties. 'Unravelling' is a worldwide string figure which is told in many different areas of the globe. The version presented on page 50 comes from India (the Assam/Burma Border) but in Germany it is about a train; carriages are added first and then the train moves away. In Africa it is called 'Stealing the Yams;' yams are dug up from the field and hung in the store to dry but a thief comes and steals them. In some places sheep are allowed to run free and the string performer says 'Baa!' as they run away. In other places it is about a mouse stealing cheeses.

5. 3D Figures

The 'Navajo Drum' (page 64) is known by almost every Navajo child. The 'Eiffel Tower' (page 63), appropriately, was taught to me in France by two ladies who wanted to see if they could remember the figures from their childhood. The 'Frog' (page 67) comes from The Guianas in South America and is a very similar figure to the 'Pig' (page 72) from New Caledonia on the other side of the Pacific Ocean.

How similar complicated figures can be known on opposite ends of the ocean is one of the mysteries posed by string figures. Did ancient peoples travel across the ocean and share their cultures or did they invent their figures independently? The intervening figure (not 3D) called 'Little Fishes' (page 67) in Melanesia is known as 'Fish,' 'Fang Trap,' 'Winding of a snake' and 'Divining Bones' in various parts of Africa.

6. Moving Figures

In the introduction to Caroline Furness Jayne's book, *String Figures and How to Make Them*, John Murdoch stated: 'the (Point Barrow) women are very fond of playing Cat's-Cradle whenever they have leisure. One favourite figure is a representation of a reindeer which is made, by moving the fingers, to run downhill from one hand to the other.' Carolyn Furness Jayne gives instructions for making an Inuit caribou but not one that runs. The version presented here might have been the way that they made this figure.

Other moving figures presented here include 'Two Fish Swimming Away' (page 80) and an Inuit 'Talking Mouth' (page 76f) which tells stories (and can bite your little finger!)

7. Other Figures

In Volume 7 of *The Bulletin of the International String Figure Association*, Tetsuo Sato from Japan presented an article called 'Olympic Flag' and subtitled it 'An Impossible String Figure.' In it he showed a method of making the flag which is only possible if the string is at one point cut and then re-tied. The following year (2001) in the next volume of the Bulletin Ronald Read of Canada showed that if the requirement that the frame strings be transverse be eliminated the impossible flag is indeed possible!

His version is presented here alongside a rabbit, a butterfly, a ringing bell and a lightning flash (see pages 86–97).

8. Partner Games

As soon as you know 'Opening A' it is possible to 'Cut the Hand' (page 99) and 'Saw' (page 98) with a partner. It has proved very useful when teaching string games to provide variety by pairing people off to practise these games. The 'Tortoise Shell' (page 104) has sometimes acted as an advertisement for string games at a festival; the figure can be made on a young child's hands and that child invariably runs off to display it to his or her parents, friends and anyone else along the way! A common sequence for 'Cat's-cradle' is presented here as well as a way of entering the sequence from 'Opening A.'

9. Tricks

The 'Thumb-Jump' (page 110) has proved to be a great way to start performances or to interest spectators before performances begin. No words are necessary. A thumb is presented to a spectator and in gestures it is suggested that he or she holds a thumb out. Then the string unwinds from the figure and jumps miraculously onto the outstretched thumb. The attached string is now in place for the next trick 'Through thumb' (page 111). Soon other children are waiting, thumbs up, for the string to jump onto their thumbs!

A wide selection of string tricks is presented here including the very simple 'Cutting the Body' (page 117) which, being so active, can be an antidote to the over concentration required by more intricate figures.

10. String Things

The Australian Aborigines were quite fond of displaying the final figure on the ground. The 'Bolivian Footprint' (page 122) comes from the Choroti people of Bolivia. Made with a normal string length the final figure resembles a human footprint. But made with a shorter or doubled loop, the final figure resembles the paw print of a wild animal.

The 'Scoubidou Man' (page 119) and the 'Wrist Watch' (page 120) were invented by my son, Raphael, and me on one of those long train and boat journeys when we had lots of time but not so much arm room. The time required to make a successful string Scoubidou Man doesn't seem to matter when sitting for long stretches on a train!

11. Children's Inventions

As soon as children start playing string games they start inventing, sharing and passing on their inventions. The 'Trampoline' (page 124) is an invented action figure that was all around the school just days after its invention during a string craze in Sussex, England, a few years ago. Many variations such as the 'Camera' and 'Kite' (see page 125) can be made from the 'Trampoline.' They are included here along with the children's inventions the 'Beard' and 'Glove' (page 126).

12. Very Simple Figures

These figures, like the 'Smile' (page 131) and the traditional 'Wasp Nest' (page 131) are so simple that they need almost no instructions. The 'Handshake' (page 130) can be a very good way to give out strings and some of the figures can provide settings for stories: Throw a doubled spinning loop into the air as the 'Sun' (page 58), then show the 'Sea' and the 'Waves running up the beach' (page 129) and you already have the setting for a story!

13. 'Stringing Stories Together'

In the 'Dragon, the Princess and Jack' (page 132) and 'Three Brothers find Treasure' (page 136) figures are woven together in such a way that the stories can be told easily while the figures are being made. The string figure, or the relevant stage in making a certain string figure, is written in brackets and inserted into the relevant part of the text. In some parts of the story almost every finger movement is accounted for and can enrich the telling

13

and showing of the story. In other parts the story takes over and there are no finger movements or figures to watch. Instructions for all the figures can be found in this book and there is ample scope for adding and improvising.

Names of Fingers and Strings

Unless otherwise instructed hands usually start and return to the 'basic position' (hold as if ready to clap).

When a loop or string goes around a finger or thumb it is named after that finger: Thumb string, Index string, Middle finger string, Ring finger string and Little finger string.

Each loop has a near string and a far string (as you look at it while the hands are held in the basic position).

When a finger has two loops the one nearest the base is the lower, the one nearer the tip is the upper.

Sometimes fingers rotate, sometimes you may drop or release a string. Check the drawing to confirm that you understand the text, and vice versa.

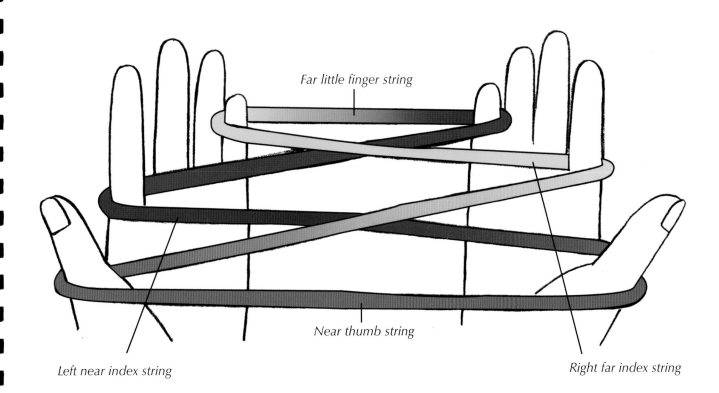

Far little finger string

Near thumb string

Left near index string

Right far index string

Following Instructions

Arrows linked around the strings denote the movement of those strings, usually by the opposite hand, as explained in the text. Arrows leading from fingers denote finger movement. When a green arrow becomes red it means that a new string has been collected by that finger.

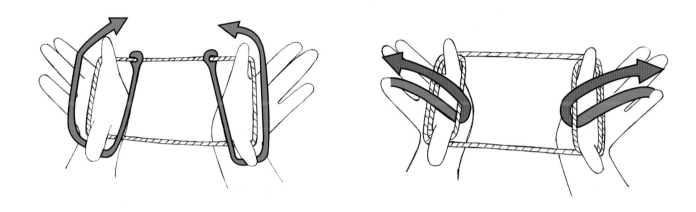

Doubling the Loop

Sometimes a shorter loop is required. This can be achieved by doubling or even trebling the loop. To double a loop, wrap one strand twice around your palm and then lift the two palm strings with the opposite hand.

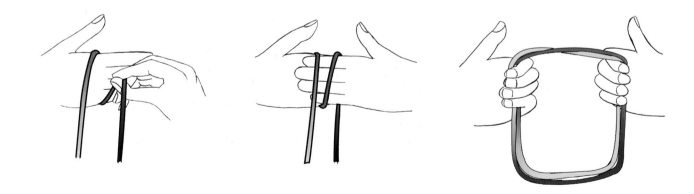

Opening A

Many figures in this book start this way.

1. Start with the hands in the 'basic position' (as if ready to clap) with the string loop on the thumbs. (String lengths are not drawn to scale). Little fingers take far thumb string from below.

2. Right index takes left palm string from below.

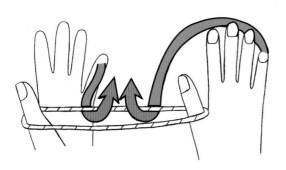

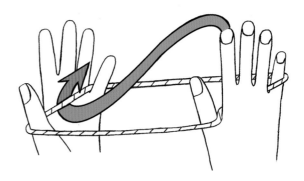

3. Left index takes right palm string from below in the centre of the palm between the index strings.

4. Now you have 'Opening A.'

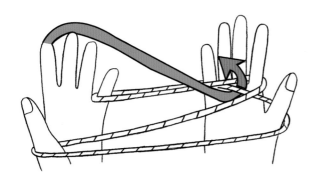

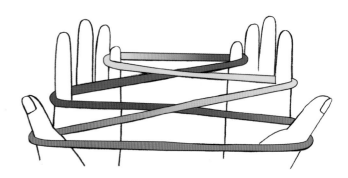

Simple Figures

Flag and girl

1&2. Hold loop as shown. Pass right-hand string to left.

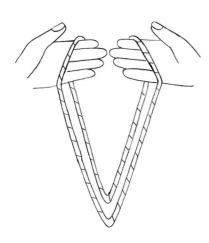 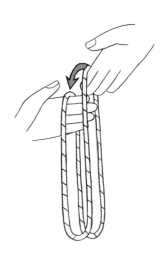

3&4. Place the four fingers of your right hand towards you, through both hanging loops.

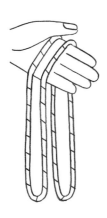 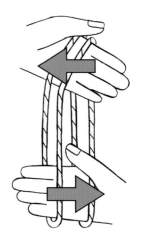

5&6. Close both hands into fists and pull apart to make the 'Flag.' Turn the right hand to 'Spot the difference!'

Flag

7&8. Again pass the right strings to the left. Hold strings with left hand to make the 'Girl' (see below).

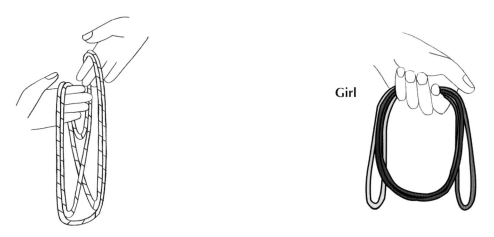

Girl

9&10. Right hand joins left and hands pull apart to make the 'Necklace.'

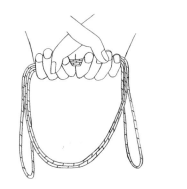

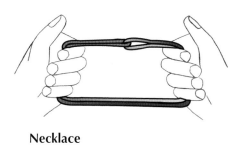

Necklace

Nibble fish

1. Put a 'Pond' on the ground. Take near part of string and turn over as shown.

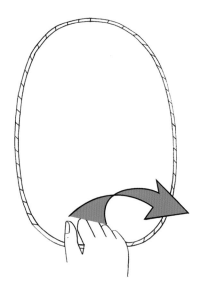

2. Put index fingers into the 'Drop' and move them apart.

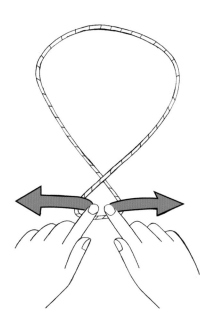

3. Give the 'Fish' a mouth!

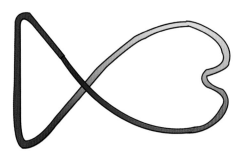

4. Turn it into an 'Eight.' Lift the lower part of the cross close to and on either side of the upper.

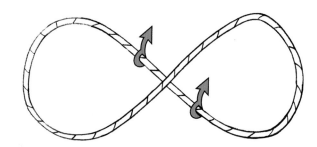

5&6. Bring hands together and apart to make the 'Jumping fish' (best with a stiff string).

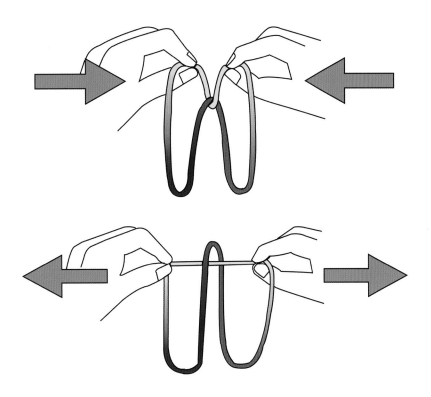

Nibble fish by Milly Reynolds

Here is a pond so round
Here is a drop that fell to the ground
Here is a bridge crossing over a stream
And here's a little nibble fish that likes to be seen
Nibble Nibble, little fish, the gnats have come to play
Nibble Nibble, little fish, that's how to spend your day
Up and down, up and down, flashing in the sun
Nibble Nibble, little fish, that's how this is done

Necklace link

1. Hold strings on index fingers.

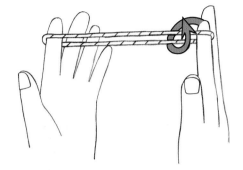

2. Rotate right index one complete turn.

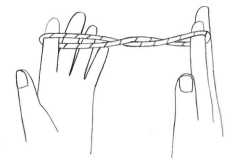

3. Place index fingers tip to tip and pass right index string onto left index finger.

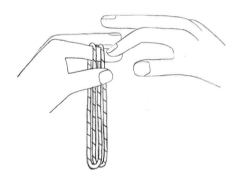

4. Place four right fingers into both hanging loops from tip side. Close right hand at base of the hanging loops.

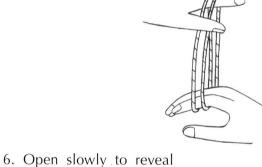

5. Release left hand. Blow on right for effect.

6. Open slowly to reveal the 'Necklace link.'

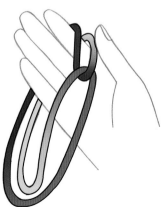

Stars

Half-second star

1. Place short or doubled loop on thumb and little finger of the left hand and on the middle finger of the right hand.

2. Right thumb tip touches right little finger tip above middle finger loop.

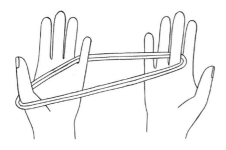 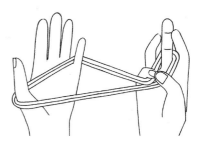

3 & 4. Turn left hand so that left fingers point to the right. Right thumb and little fingers, still touching, move down the right fingers and under the right palm string, then the hands and fingers are straightened out and placed together.

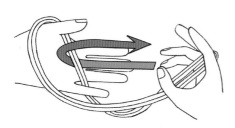 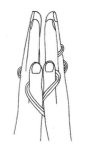

5. Open hands to display the half-second star, so named because, once learned, that is how long it takes to make! For best effect it should be displayed vertically, right hand on top.

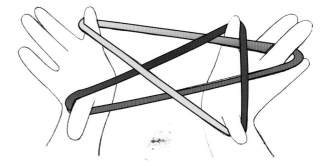

Five-pointed star (1)

1. Place short, doubled or trebled loop on little fingers. Right index enters the little finger loop from below (from base of little fingers). Right index describes a clockwise semi-circle pointing towards the left palm in order to straighten up (keep right little finger pointing forwards so it doesn't drop its loop).

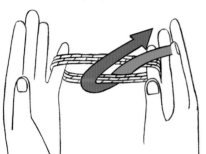

2. Left index shares right index loop from below.

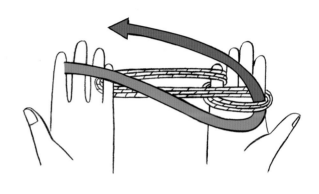

3. Right thumb over index strings, lifts near little finger string.

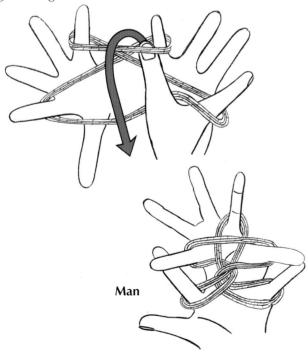

Man

4. Hold hands out to show the 'star.'

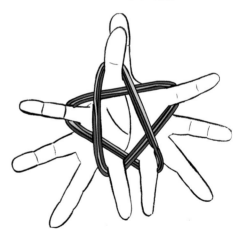

5. Hold right hand vertically (as if waving) and twist left hand clockwise horizontally (like a plate) to see a 'Man.'

Five-pointed star (2)

1&2. Make Opening A with a short, doubled or trebled loop.

3. Release thumbs.

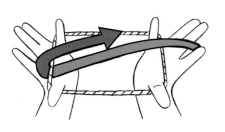
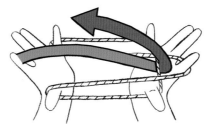
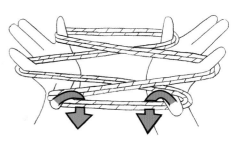

4. Thumbs, over index loops, take little finger loops from above. (Drawing shows tips touching so loops can slip from little fingers to thumbs) Release little fingers.

5. Little fingers, over index loops, take far thumb strings from below.

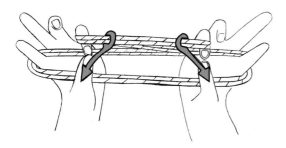
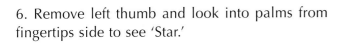
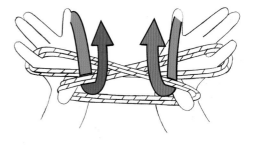

6. Remove left thumb and look into palms from fingertips side to see 'Star.'

7. Hold right hand vertically and twist left hand clockwise horizontally (like a plate) to see a 'Man.'

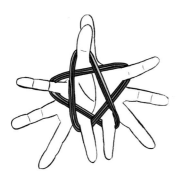
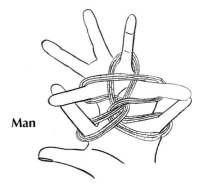

Man

Navajo star

1&2. Place loop on thumbs and index with an away-turn twist (see how string should look in the drawing) on the left palm. Right index finger and thumb enter (as shown by arrows) and return. Repeat on right with an away-turn twist (see second drawing) in one of the two thumb/index strings.

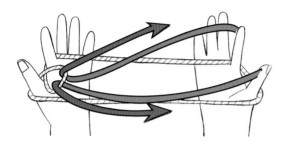 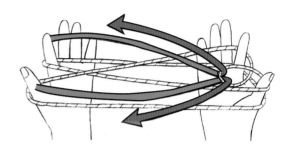

3. Little fingers move over index loops to pull back far thumb strings from below. Release thumb strings.

4. Thumbs lift near index strings to display the 'Navajo star'.

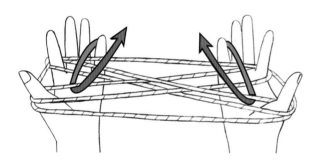 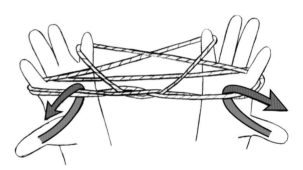

Pole star

1&2. Make Opening A.

3. Rotate first little fingers, then thumbs, each moving first towards the centre of the figure.

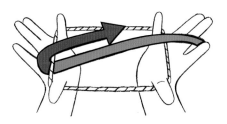 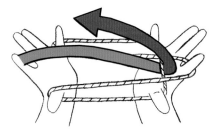 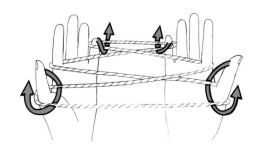

4. Thumbs move down through index loops, pick up near little finger string and return up through index loops.

5. Likewise, little fingers move down through index loops, pick up far thumb string and return.

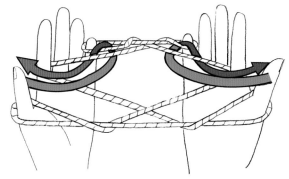 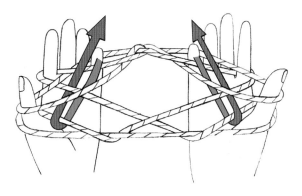

5. Release index finger.

6. Display the 'Pole star' on the hands or on the ground.

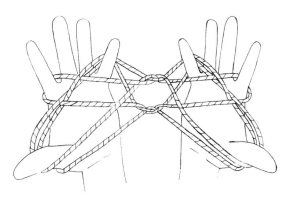 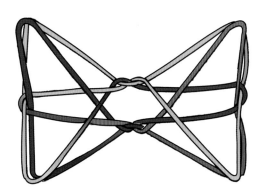

27

Elastic band star

1. Put elastic band on left index and thumb. Right index moves under palm-side line and over back line which it hooks back over palm.

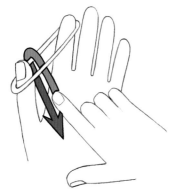

2. Right index then gives the line a half turn clockwise.

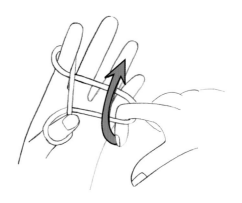

3. The loop is placed on the left little finger.

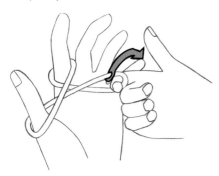

4. Right middle finger hooks back shared left thumb/index line.

5&6. Right index hooks palm line (near to little finger) and pulls it up through the stretched loop.

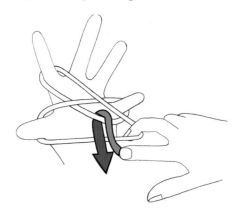

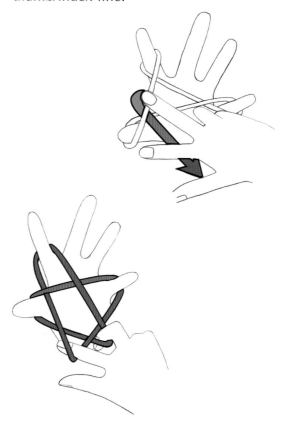

28

Crossed-hands star

1. Place short, doubled or trebled string on little fingers. Rotate right little finger around its own strings (anticlockwise).

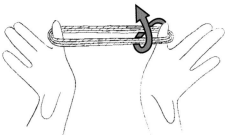

2. Right index goes up into right little finger loop, over far string and returns below.

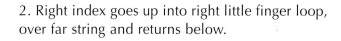
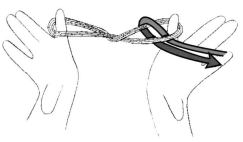

3. Right thumb, over index strings picks up right near little finger string.

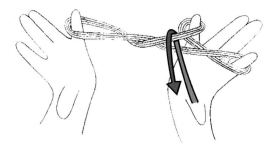

4. Left index, over other strings, picks up right far little finger string.

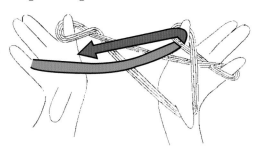

5. Left index rotates around its own strings (anti-clockwise).

6&7. Turn hands so that left thumb moves under all strings to rest next to right thumb as wrists cross.

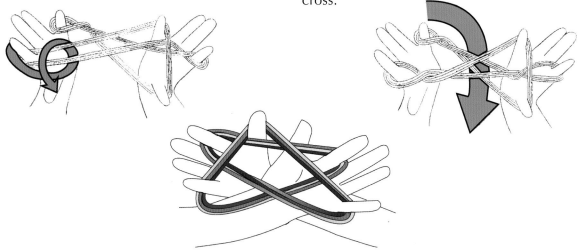

Star in a star

Use elastic band, doubled or short string.

1. Place loop over left thumb and little finger. Pull out back string UNDER palm-string, twist clockwise.

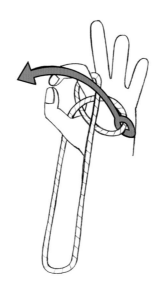

2. Place twist over index and thumb.

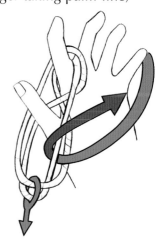

3. Pull down thumb loops until they are even. Put palm line on little finger. (Drawing shows little finger taking palm-line)

4. Pinch left thumb to index. Lift shared string off thumb and index and drop on the palm side.

5&6. Secure string on fingers with right hand as shown while left thumb releases string and takes thumb-side middle line instead.

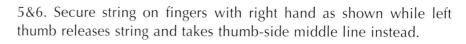

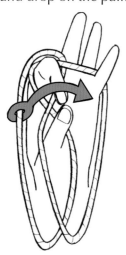

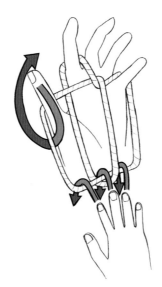

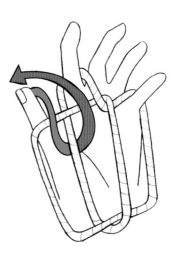

7. Twist palm string and pull it down below the base of the left little and thumb loops.

8. Right middle and index take left little and thumb loops and pull them through the twisted loop for 'Star in a star.' (Right thumb can temporarily help by holding the twisted loop wide).

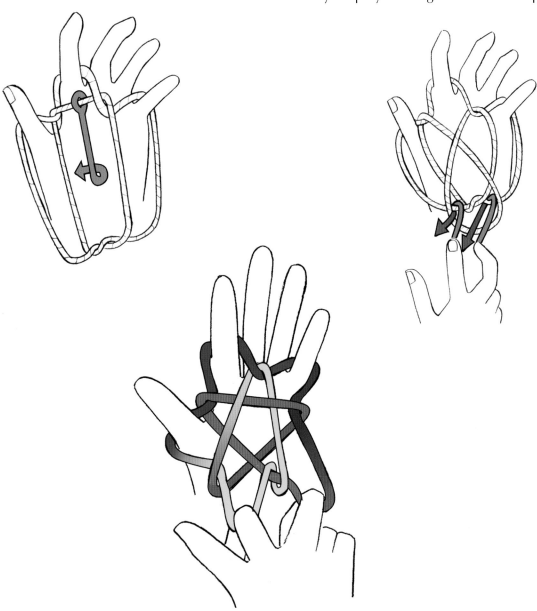

Five person star

1. Put six strings on the ground arranged as a 'Sun' with five rays.

2. Push the 'Rays' under the edge of the 'Sun.'

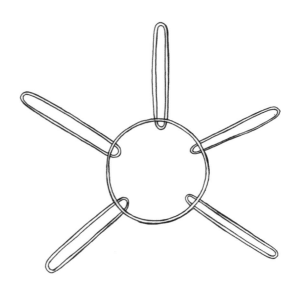

3. Each person hooks both ends of the 'Sun's rays' with index fingers.

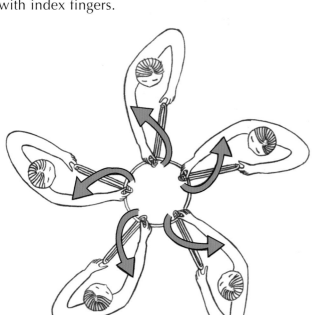

4. Bring hands together.

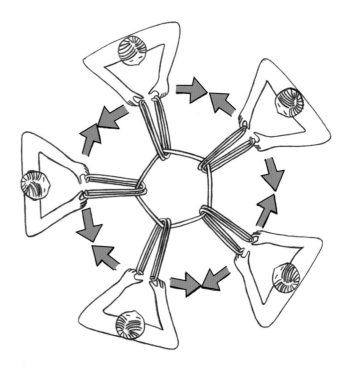

5. Take hands and see what happens! Now try with more people.

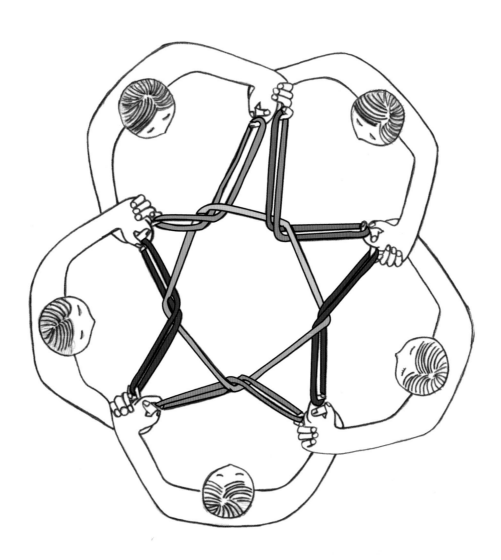

Big star

1. Make Opening A. Thumbs get far little finger strings from below (after going over own far strings, down through index loops and below near little finger strings).

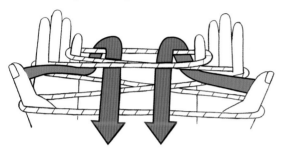

2. Middle fingers, over index loops, get far thumb strings from below. Release thumbs (not shown).

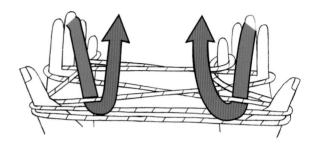

3. Thumbs, over near index string, under everything else, get far little finger string from below. Release little fingers (not shown).

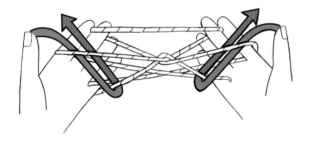

4. Thumbs, over index loops, under near middle strings, get far middle strings from below. Release middle fingers (not shown).

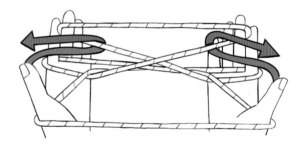

5. Index fingers, over near index strings, get far thumb strings from below.

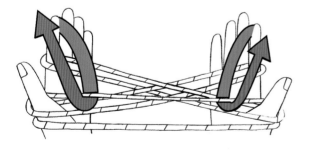

6. Index fingers, over top far index strings, down through lower loops, allow lower loops to slip off.

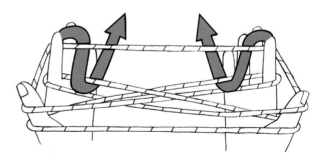

7. Middle and ring fingers pinch near lower thumb string after going below all strings except the upper thumb string.

8. Pinched string is brought down through thumb loop.

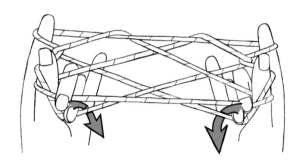

9. Release thumbs. Thumbs retake middle finger string from base of middle finger for the 'Big star.'

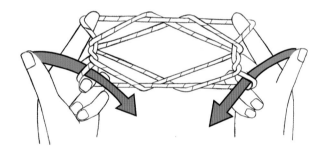

10. Place a second string above the first and then lift lower strings over upper and off the fingers.

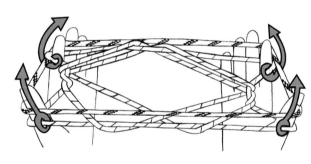

11. Display with the help of a second person (or elbows as shown here).

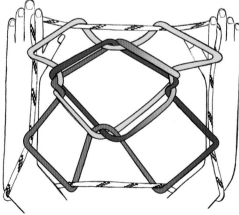

Popular Figures

Cup and saucer, Witch's hat, Rabbit's ears, Eiffel Tower and Sock on the line

1&2. Make Opening A.

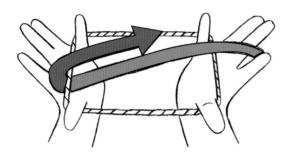
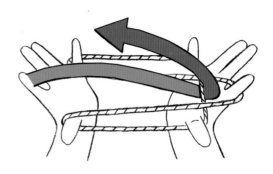

3. Thumbs over own far thumb string and near index string take far index from below and return.

4,5&6. Lower thumb string is lifted by teeth or opposite hand (figure a) over upper thumb string (figure b) and off the finger (figure c).

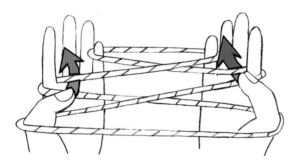
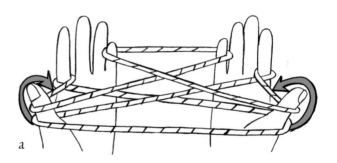

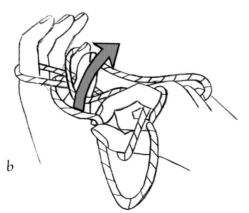
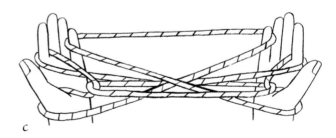

7. Release little fingers for 'Cup and saucer.'

8. Take near thumb string with teeth (use a clean string or ask someone to lift it for you) for 'Witch's hat.' (For 'Rabbit's ears,' not shown, put hands on head, face in the big triangle and mouth string goes under chin).

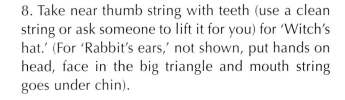

Witch's hat

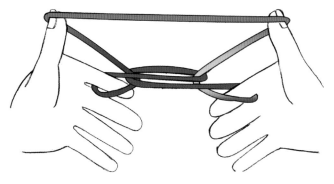

Cup and saucer

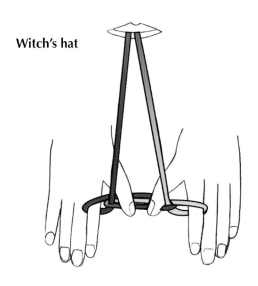

9. Release thumbs for 'Eiffel Tower.'

10. Release mouth strings for 'Sock on the line.' Pull apart and it disappears.

Eiffel Tower

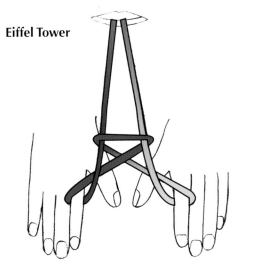

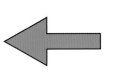
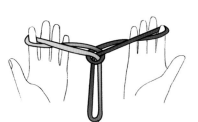
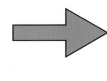

Sock on the line

Jacob's ladder and Cat's whiskers

1&2. Make Opening A.

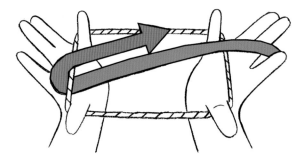

3. Release thumbs.

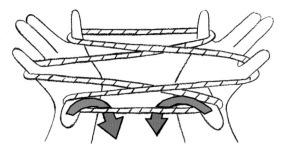

4. Thumbs go under intervening strings, below far string and return with it (far little finger string).

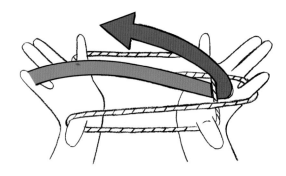

5. Thumbs go over first string (near index) to pick up second string (far index) from below. Release little fingers.

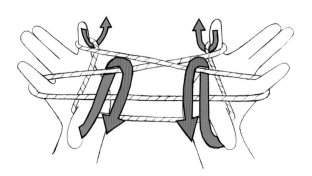

6. Little fingers go over first string (index) to pick up second (far thumb) from below. Release thumbs.

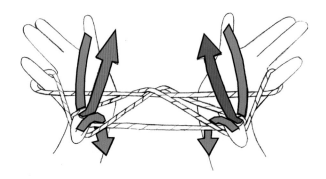

7. This is 'cat's whiskers.' Thumbs go over two whiskers (index strings) to pick up next string (near little finger) from below.

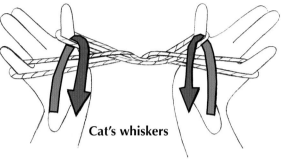

Cat's whiskers

8. Thumbs share index loop (near index) from below.

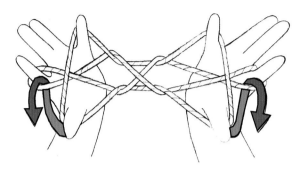

9. Lower thumb loop is lifted over upper and off the thumb. (Thumb can dip under near string to achieve this as shown in the drawing).

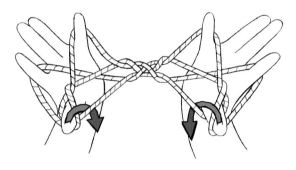

10. Carefully release little fingers (do not pull apart).

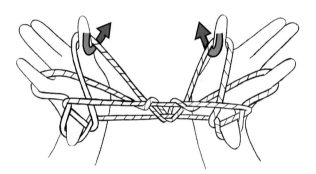

11&12. Index fingers point down into triangles at base of thumbs. Index fingers keep pointing down and move under all strings, pointing out and away. Holding palms away at arms' length can help form 'Jacob's ladder.'

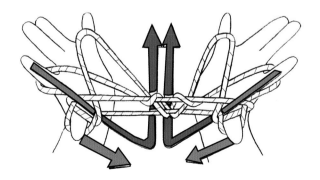

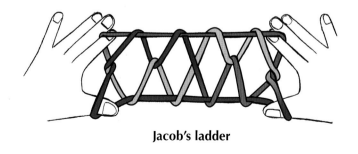

Jacob's ladder

Apache door

1&2. Place loop on thumbs and little fingers. Whole hands (even thumbs) enter palm strings from below.

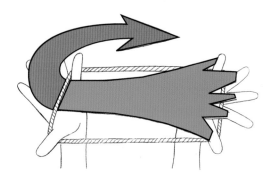 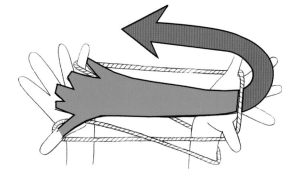

3. Thumbs take near little finger strings from below.

4. Little fingers take far thumb strings from below.

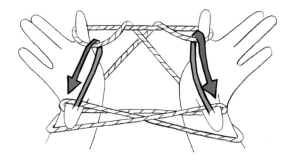

5. Right hand passes between left thumb and index to 'grab' left wrist.

6. Note upper left thumb string pair. This will need to be temporarily held between right thumb and index.

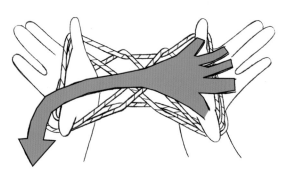 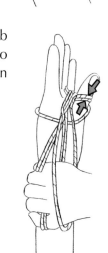

7&8. Right thumb and index holds upper thumb pair while left thumb retreats from all its strings (not wrist string) and then enters again into held pair (this time over intervening strings). Release held strings. Repeat on other hand.

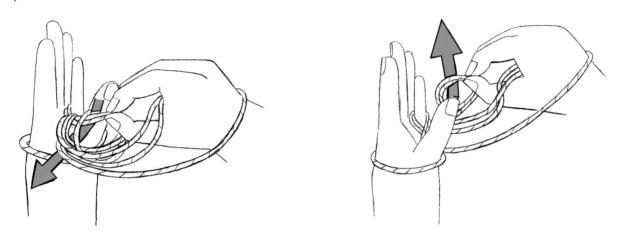

9&10. Opposite hands lift back of wrist strings over fingers and drop into centre of figure to make the 'Apache door.'

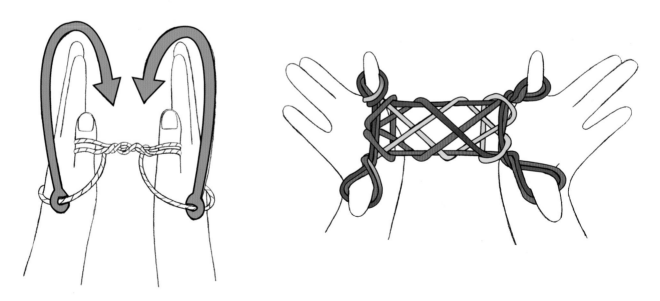

Parachute, Scissors and Broom

1. Hold loop on left thumb and little finger with one segment on the palm and the rest hanging in front of the forearm. Pull palm string out with other hand (in front of hanging loop, which becomes the next palm string).

2. Pull new palm string out with other hand (through hanging loop which becomes a palm string).

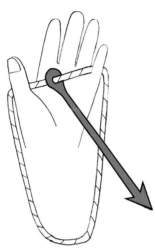

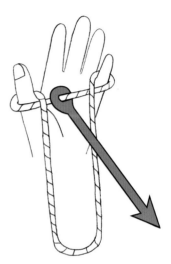

3&4. Right hand enters hanging loop. Thumb enters thumb loop and index enters little finger loop (both from above). Right thumb and index tips touch below central palm strings (far thumb and near little finger) to form a 'ring.' This 'ring' is pulled under lowest palm string and out through the hanging loop to make the 'Scissors.'

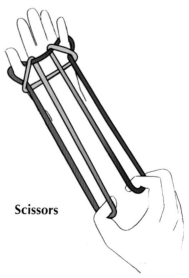

Scissors

5. Hook left index over own palm strings into right thumb loop. Hook left middle over own palm strings between long loops. Hook left ring over own palm strings into right index loop. Right hand places both loops to the back of the left wrist.

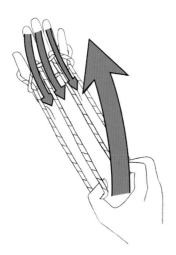

6&7. Right index lifts single upper centre palm string for 'Broom' or ...

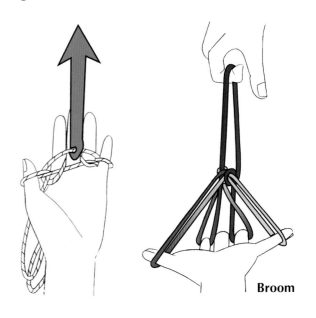

Broom

8&9. Right index lifts both centre palm strings for the 'Parachute.' Hold left hand uppermost to show the parachute falling from the sky.

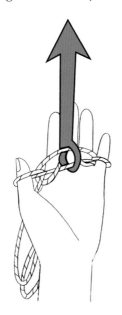

Parachute

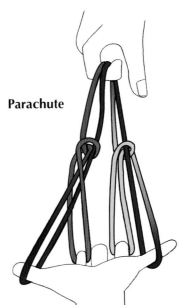

The flying bird

1. Make 'Scissors' (page 42). Note two triangles and a square on the left palm. Release right hand.

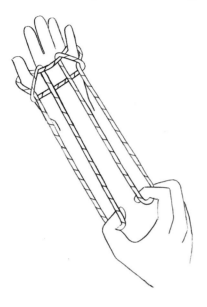

2. Right thumb takes base of left thumb triangle from below (and from inside thumb hanging loop). Right little finger takes base of left little finger triangle from below (and from inside other hanging loop). Right index takes top of square (centre of top palm string) from below.

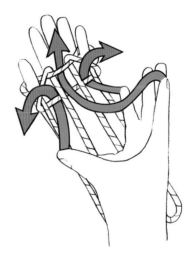

3. Pull right hand out. Wiggle right fingers to tighten knots a little.

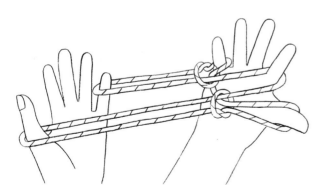

4. Release right thumb and little fingers to free the 'wings.' Pull apart to make the 'Flying bird' fly from right to left.

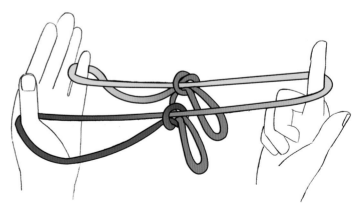

The mosquito

From Hawaii. It is known as 'The Locust' in Uganda and 'The Fly' in the Solomon Islands and Guyana.

1. Place loop on middle fingers. Opposite hands wrap strings around four fingers in opposite directions.

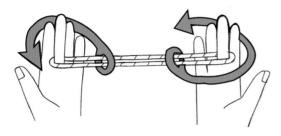

2. Right little finger takes two left middle finger strings from below.

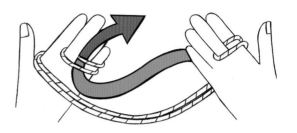

3. Left little finger takes two middle finger strings from below.

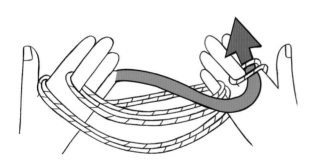

4. Lift back of wrist strings off both hands.

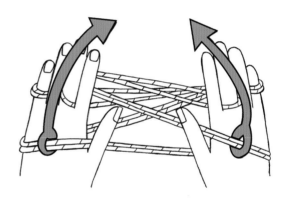

5. Pull hands apart to tighten knot.

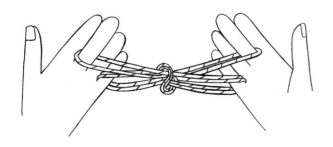

6. Hands come slightly together. Release little fingers to show 'Mosquito.' Pull hands apart to make 'mosquito' disappear.

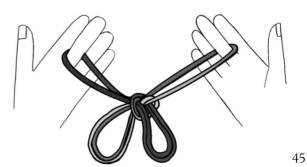

Fish spear

1. Place loop on thumbs and little fingers. Right index takes left palm string from below.

2. Rotate right index around its own strings. Make sure that the resulting twist is in the string and not around the finger.

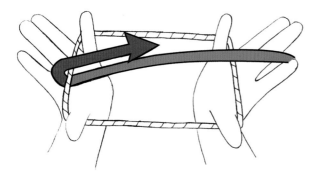

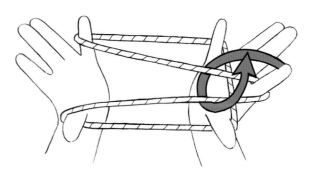

3. Left index takes right palm string from below (through twisted index loop).

4. Release right thumb and little finger and pull apart for 'Fish spear' (see opposite page).

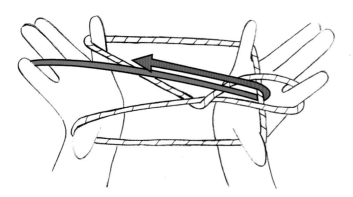

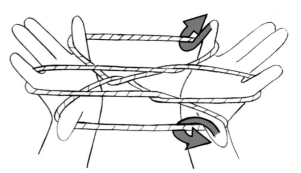

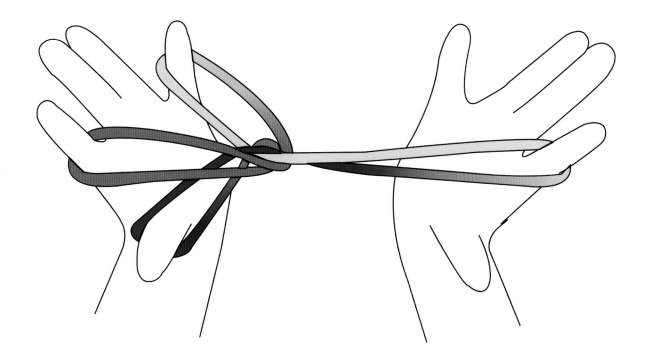

An international String Figure: the people of the Torres Straits (north of Australia) call it a 'Fish Spear,' in Alaska it is a 'Duck Spear,' in Africa a 'Palm Tree' and the Native Americans call it 'Pitching a Tent.'

Stories

The blinking eye. *A story by Jaimen McMillan*

Once upon a willow tree ...
An owl wrapped one claw around one branch (1)
And the other, upon another. (2)
She yawned widely ... (3&4)
Folded her first wing across her chest, then the same with the next (6&7)
She blinked three times. (8&9)
WHOO! WHOO! WHOO!
And fell fast asleep.

1&2. Place loop over left index. The hanging strings represent long willow leaves. Take far string. Wrap it over index (the 'First branch') and then lay it over thumb (the 'Second branch').

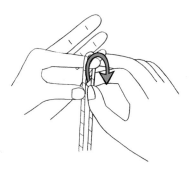 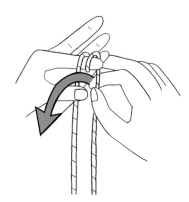

3&4. Stretch top index loop so that it is shared with the thumb. The act of widening the loop represents 'Yawning.'

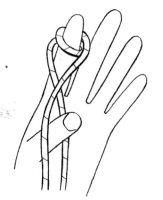 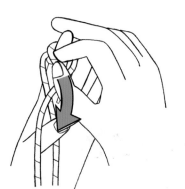

5,6&7. The two hanging thumb strings must be lifted over the thumb in opposite directions, the wrist-side string onto the palm-side and the palm-side string onto the wrist side. These movements represent 'folding the wings'.

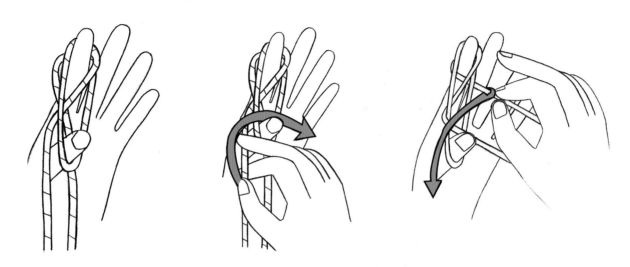

8&9. Keep index, thumb and hanging strings in one line. Keep index loops at tip of index. Press left middle finger against index loops. Pull on hanging strings to make the 'Eye' open and close.

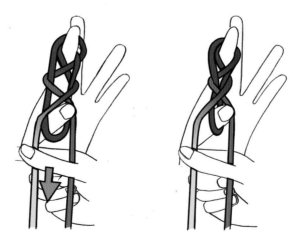

Unravelling. *A story from the Lushai Hills*

A man was worried about the safety of his wife and his ox. Especially his ox! Before he left home to go to work he fenced his house securely to keep them safe. Around five stakes he tied a strong rope. Now they would be safe. But while he was away a fire broke out. "Oh no! My poor wife! My poor ox!"

He ran home to untie the fence to free his wife and ox. He lifted the loop from one end and pulled the other. No good! It just got tighter! Just then the wise one of the village was passing by ... and only just in time! "Don't pull this one! Pull the other one!" the wise one cried. The man did and the rope came free!

1&2. Place loop over left hand placed on edge, thumb upmost. Right index (palm-side at join of left thumb and index) hooks back string and rotating clockwise places it (fingertip to fingertip) on the index.

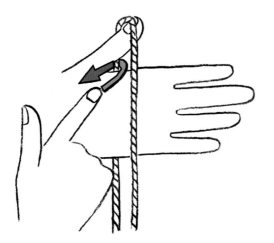 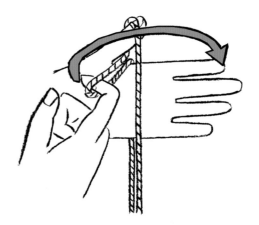

3&4. Right index (palm-side at join of index and middle) hooks back-string and rotating clockwise places it on the middle.

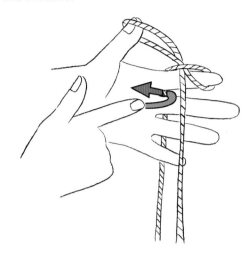 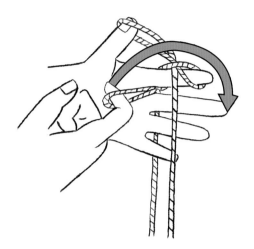

5. Repeat with other fingers.

6. Take off thumb loop. If the far string is pulled it is only tightened.

7. The other string needs to be pulled to free the fingers.

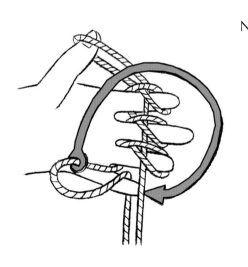

Not this ...

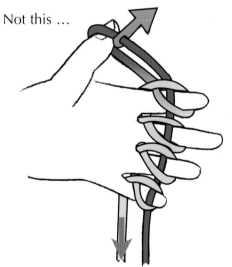

This!

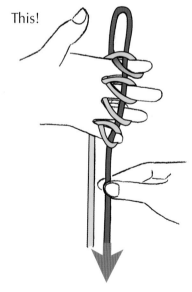

The Sealskin House. *A story by Milly Reynolds using the 'Siberian House'*

> My house is made from the skin of the seal (1-4)
> I hunt with my spear through the ice field (5)
> I hang up the skins until they are dry (6)
> And then build my house under the sky.

1&2. Place loop on thumbs and little fingers. Right index, middle and ring fingers take left palm string from below. Left index, middle and ring fingers take right palm string from below.

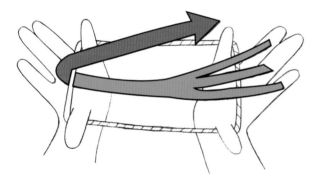 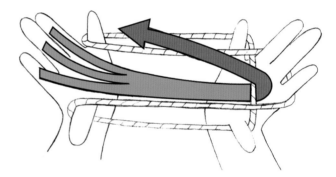

3&4. Turn palms to face you. Close fingers over all strings except the nearest, then bring hands together so that near string hangs loosely. Throw string over the fists to the back. This thrown string is the 'Sealskin.'

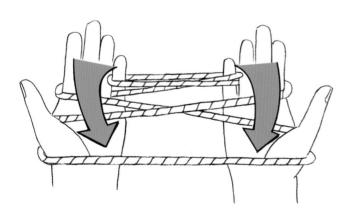 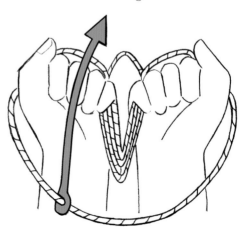

5. Open hands and check that triangles below index are easily seen. Thumbs plunge into these triangles (the 'Ice field'), go below lowest far string and raise it through the triangles.

6. Opposite hands (one at a time) lift lowest back-of-hand-string off all four fingers to drop on the palm side making the 'Sealskin house.'

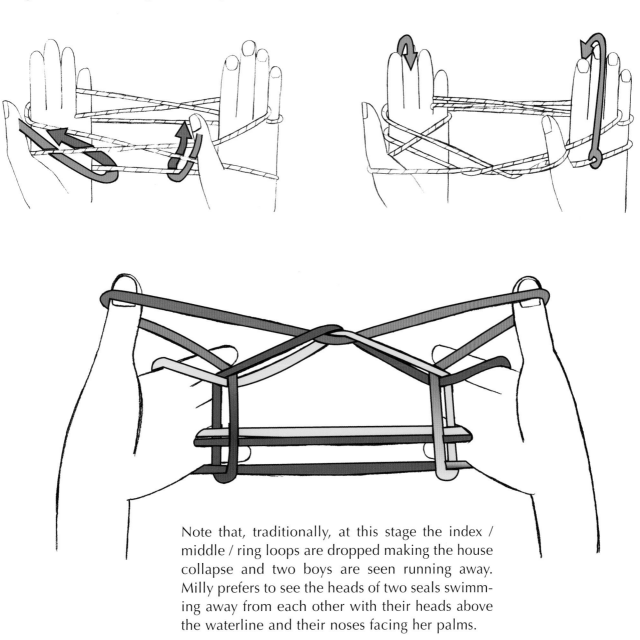

Note that, traditionally, at this stage the index / middle / ring loops are dropped making the house collapse and two boys are seen running away. Milly prefers to see the heads of two seals swimming away from each other with their heads above the waterline and their noses facing her palms.

The Straw House. A story by Milly Reynolds using the African Grass Hut

I went for a walk to visit a friend (1&2)
I went over and under and round the bend (3,4&5)
She lives in a house(6&7)
That is made out of straw
She said, "Do take a banana …
But don't take them all!"

1&2. Place loop on left thumb and little finger. Pass right hand through hanging loop, under the palm, around the back to take the palm string by the left thumb. Bring this string back through hanging loop and place on the left index.

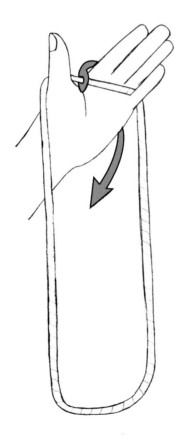
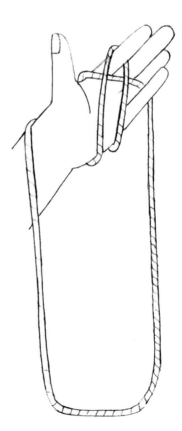

54

3&4. Put the string which is squeezed between left ring and little finger onto thumb. (Don't take it off the little finger.) In the drawing this is shown by the movement of the thumb.

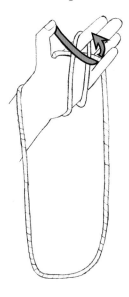
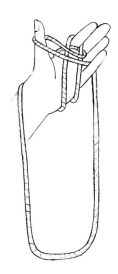

5. Turn hand over. Lift central string off over all four fingers. Keep hold of this string.

6. Pull this string away from the left palm with a gentle sawing motion.

7. Hold the 'Straw house' as shown.

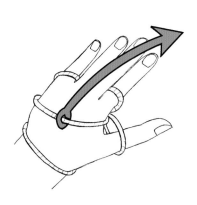
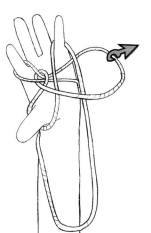
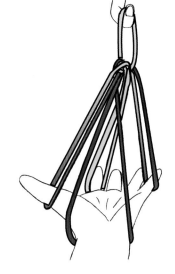

8. Remove left hand and hold out a bunch of four bananas. Say, 'Take a banana.' When a friend takes a banana all of them disappear and the friend is called 'Greedy!'

Disappearing mouse

Mice are scurrying about, (1-4)
Under leaves and twigs. (5-8)
Here's a mouse with two big ears, (9)
Make a sound and it disappears!

1. Put loop on left little finger and across left palm. Left ring finger over upper palm string takes lower palm string.

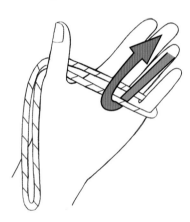

2. Repeat with middle finger.

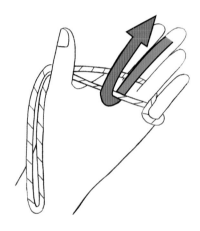

3. Repeat with index finger.

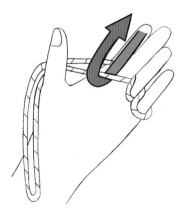

4. Lay loop untwisted around thumb and back on palm.

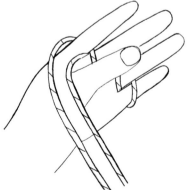

56

5. Left index finger over upper palm string takes lower palm string.

6. Repeat with middle finger.

7. Repeat with ring finger.

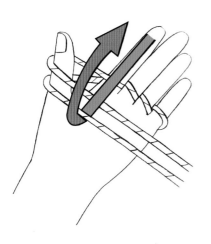 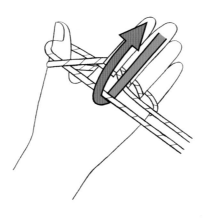 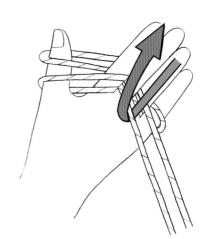

8. Repeat with little finger. Remove thumb loops and hold strings in left fist as 'Mouse.'

9. Pull 'tail' downwards, strings pass through fingers and 'mouse' disappears.

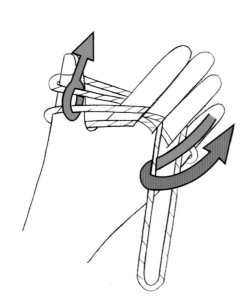 

Birthday party

Once there was a Birthday Party. First, balloons were made. Then, the tablecloth was shaken and put on the table.

1&2. Double the loop and throw it in the air to make the 'Balloon.'

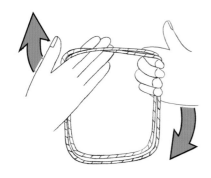

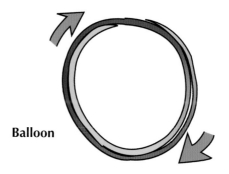

Balloon

3&4. Place loop on thumbs and little fingers. Thumbs move over far strings and return underneath. This is the 'Tablecloth' and can be 'shaken.'

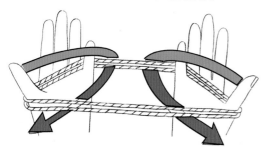

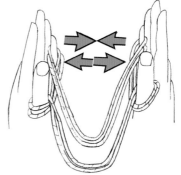

5&6. Thumbs move over near strings and under far strings with which they return to make the 'Table.'

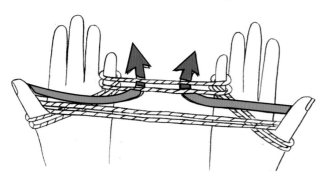

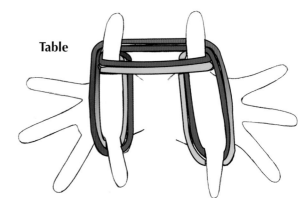

Table

> A cake was brought in and the candles were lit ...
> and blown out.

7. Move 'table-legs' together to make the 'Cake.' Note that drawings in this sequence which show thumbs uppermost are drawn from the point of view of the spectator.

Cake

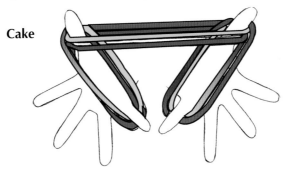

8,9&10. Little fingers take palm-side thumb strings from below. This is the 'unlit candle.' Note that each hand has four upper palm strings and two lower palm strings. To make the 'lit candle' temporarily push two lower palm strings between index and middle. Blow and release to extinguish flame.

Lit candle

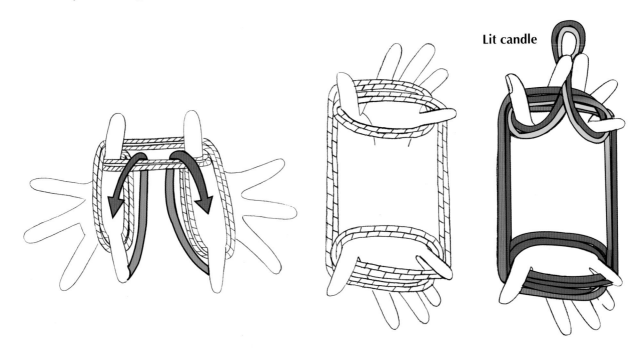

Music played and games went on until the stars came out.

11&12. Index fingers dive into space on own palm to lift double lower palm strings. Little fingers and thumbs dip under long strings connecting the two hands. These strings should slip off if strings are kept taut as fingers point to each other.

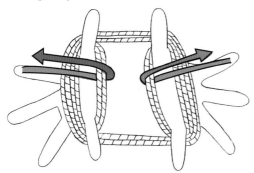 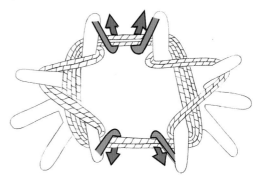

13&14. Splay fingers apart then together to make the 'Accordion'

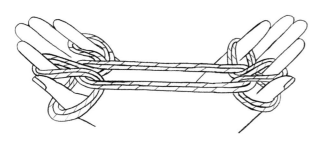 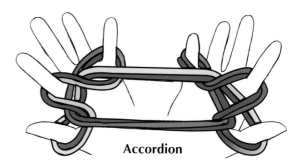

Accordion

15,16&17. Swap index loops to make the 'Star.' (Make sure one loop goes through the other).

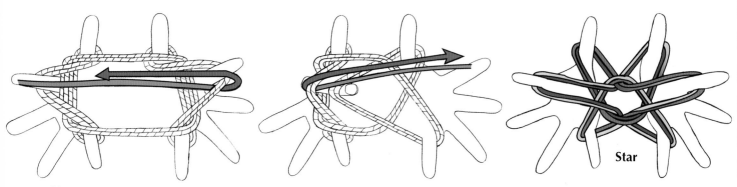

Star

> Then everyone went home with a party gift. Mine was a pair of sunglasses!

18,19&20. Place index loops untwisted on thumbs (don't pull apart). Release little finger loops and pass all thumb loops to the little, ring and middle fingers, tip first, making the 'Party gift.'

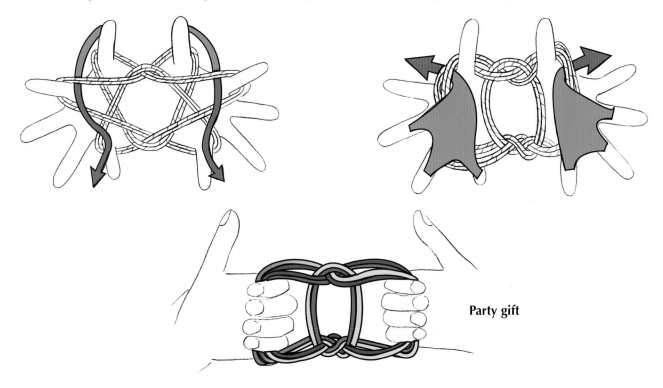

Party gift

21&22. Place index and thumbs over outer strings, under inner and up into the centre. Release outer strings and open centre to form the 'Sunglasses.'

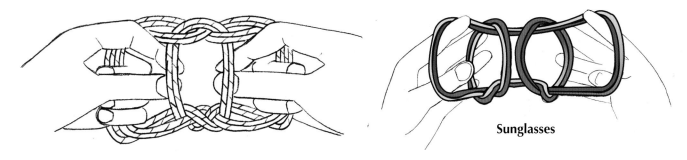

Sunglasses

Man and bed A 'Kamut Song' (string figure song) from Murray Island in the Torres Straits

Man on a bed, man on a bed, lies asleep, lies asleep … bed breaks!

1. Make Opening A. Thumbs, over own far strings and under index strings, collect near little finger strings from below.

2. Little fingers (and ring fingers can help) go down through index loops to get far thumb strings from below.

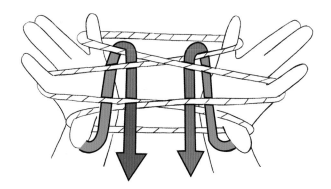

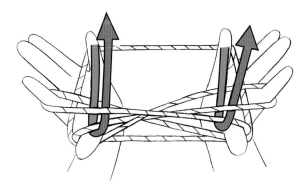

3. Release index fingers for 'man on a bed.' Drop little fingers, pull apart and the 'bed breaks.'

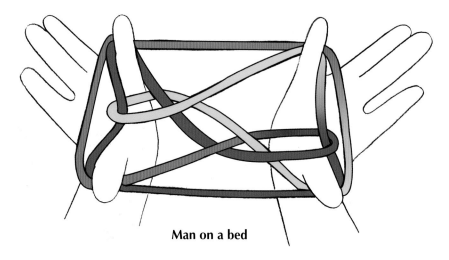

Man on a bed

3D Figures

Eiffel tower on four feet

1. Place the loop on your thumbs and index fingers in the basic position.

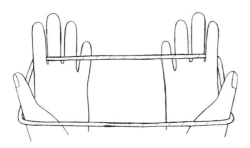

2. Put 'rings' on your left index and thumb. Use your right hand to do this.

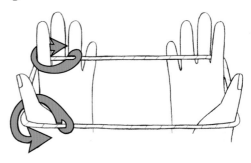

3. Right index and thumb enter left index and thumb loops from below (share 'rings') and return.

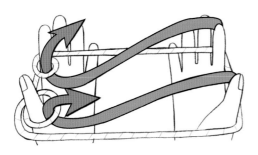

4. Lift the two central strings straight upwards with your teeth (figure a) — use a clean string or ask someone to lift it for you — while pointing index and thumbs down through the middle and spreading them out like the feet of the 'Eiffel Tower' (figure b).

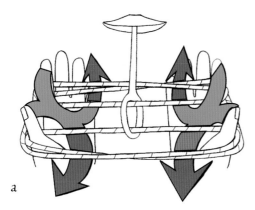

a

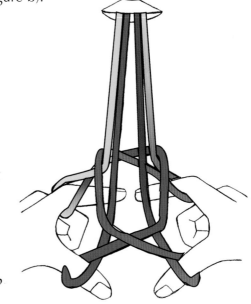

b

The Navajo drum

1. Place loop crossed around wrists as shown.

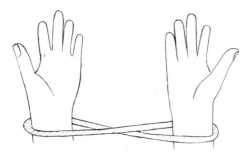

2. Wrap near string around wrists as shown. Use opposite hands to do this.

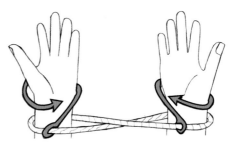

3&4. Thumb and little finger take front of wrist string from below. Repeat on the other side.

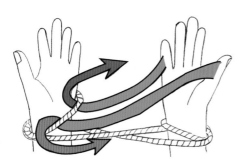

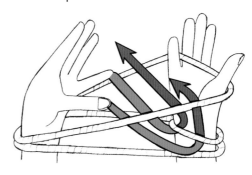

5&6. Middle finger takes palm string from below. Repeat on other side.

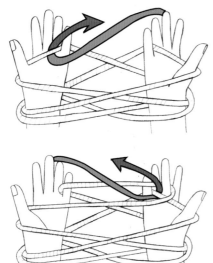

7. Hold the 'Drum' as shown.

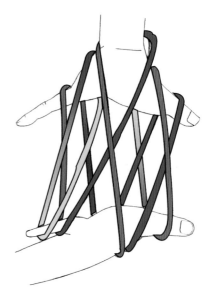

The tepee

1. Place loop on left thumb and index and pull short link between thumb and index down between forearm and hanging loop.

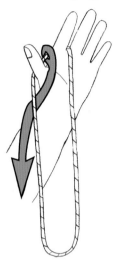

2. Place right hand in the hanging loop in front of (on top of) the string coming from the thumb and behind (under) the string coming down from the index.

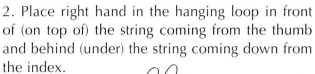

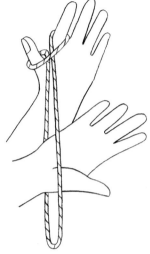

3. Right thumb and little finger go over short left palm string to enter downwards into back of thumb and index loops respectively. Right thumb and little finger then straighten up and return with these strings.

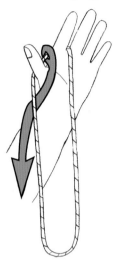

4. Right hand descends so that right palm forms base of the 'Tepee.'

The Navajo butterfly

1. Place index fingers in small twist as shown. Thumbs lift lower part of loop as shown.

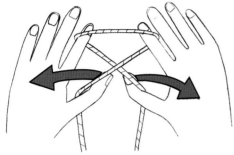

2. Rotate index fingers five times around their own loops (drawing shows only three times).

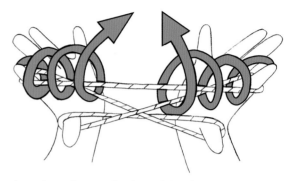

3. Middle fingers enter index loops from below to push near index strings down through thumb loops. Thumbs release their loops onto this pushed string.

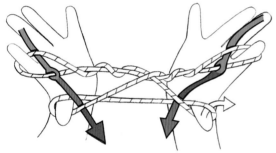

4. Thumbs take pushed middle finger strings from middle fingers.

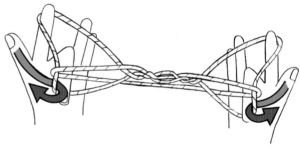

5. Give right hand strings to left hand (thumb to thumb, index to index).

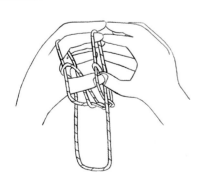

6. Right hand takes left thumb strings from tip side. Left fingers take left index strings from tip side.

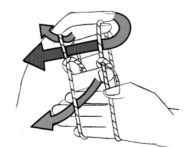

7. Display as shown with thumbs removing near top strings to make the 'Butterfly' open and close its wings.

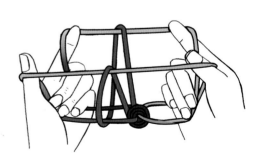

Little fishes and frog

1. Place doubled loop on index and arrange so that parallel strings are on near side. Thumbs move over lower parallel string under lower part of cross, over upper parallel string and under upper part of cross.

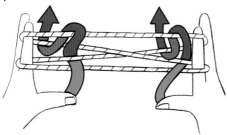

2&3. Little fingers bend over straight near index string (figure a) and over diagonal string which is hooked back. Little fingers lift up straight near index string (figure b).

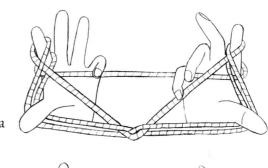

a

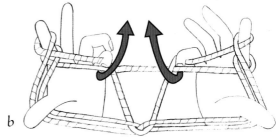

b

4. Index fingers bend down into little finger loops and lift up near little finger string in centre of figure.

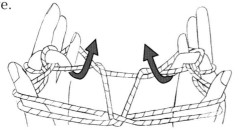

5. Release thumbs and a 'W' figure flashes into existence. (This in the Pacific Islands is 'Little Fishes' and in various parts of Africa is 'Fish,' 'Fang Trap,' 'Winding of the Snake' and 'Diving Bones.')

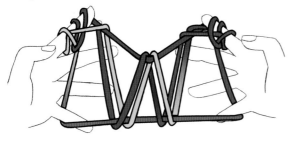

Little fishes

6. Thumbs re-take released strings (double strings which enter and leave 'W'). Release triple index loops and pull apart.

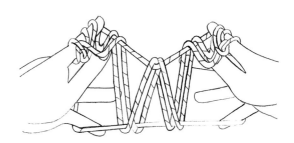

7. Index fingers bend down into little finger loops and lift up near little finger string in centre of figure. Release thumbs.

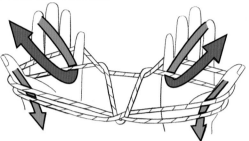

8. Thumbs enter little finger loops from below and continue in a rotating motion down and back with the far little finger strings.

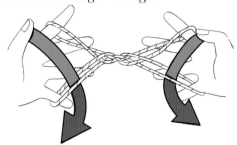

9, 10,11&12. Thumb loops are lifted off thumbs, up through index loops, and then are replaced on thumbs. Little finger loops are likewise lifted off little fingers, up through index loops, and then are replaced on little fingers (see figures a–d). Note: In drawings only move of left thumb loop is shown. Repeat with right hand.

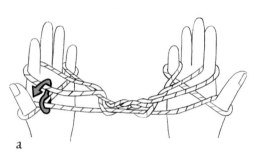

a

b

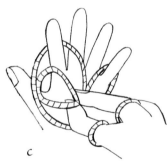

c

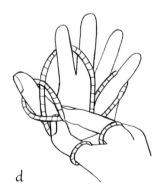

d

13. Index loops are lifted off index fingers and placed over the whole hands so becoming a wrist loop. (In drawing only left hand index loop move is shown.) Repeat with right hand.

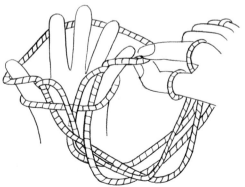

14. Place right thumb loop on left thumb and place right little finger loop on left little finger.

15. Carefully remove right hand from right wrist loop.

16. Right little, ring and middle fingers remove left thumb loops from tip side and right index removes left little finger loops from tip side. Carefully remove left hand from left wrist loop.

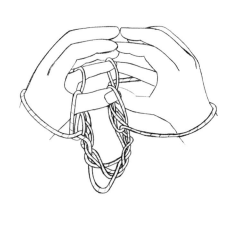
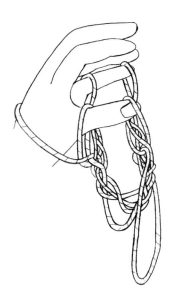
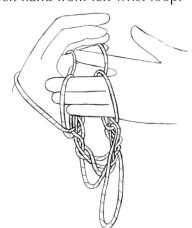

17,18&19. Left fingers remove right index loops. Display the 'Frog' in various ways as shown.

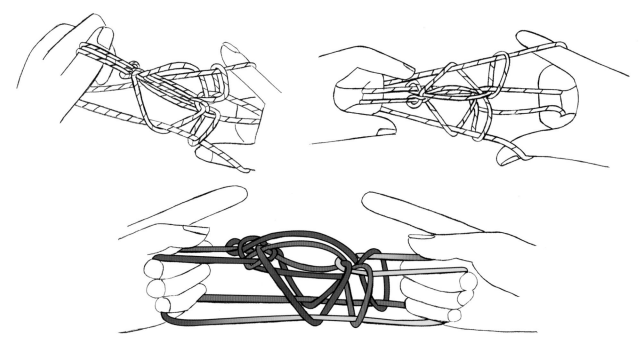

69

Bird's nest and racing car

1. Hold loop on left little finger, left thumb and right little finger. Right index and thumb, pinching together, enter left palm string from above, then stretch wide apart as they turn upwards to straighten.

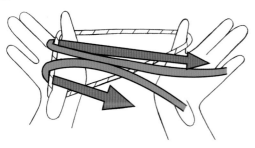

2. Left index takes right far index string from below.

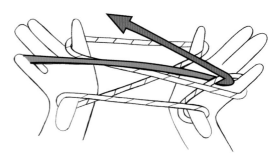

3. Thumbs, over index loops, take near little finger strings.

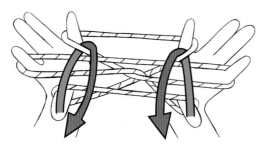

4. Middle fingers, over index loops, take far thumb strings which are held high between middle fingers and index. Release thumb strings and little finger strings.

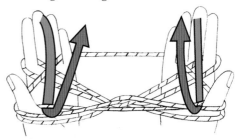

5&6. Ring fingers and little fingers hook down far index strings and thumbs lift up near index strings for the 3D Navajo figure, the 'Bird's nest.'

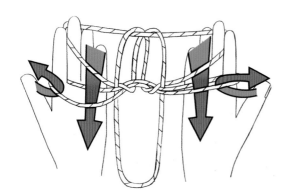

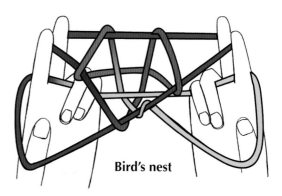

Bird's nest

7. Release right middle finger. Right middle finger carefully shares left middle loop by taking far middle finger string from below.

8&9. Right index lifts far middle string for the 'Racing car' (not strictly 3D).

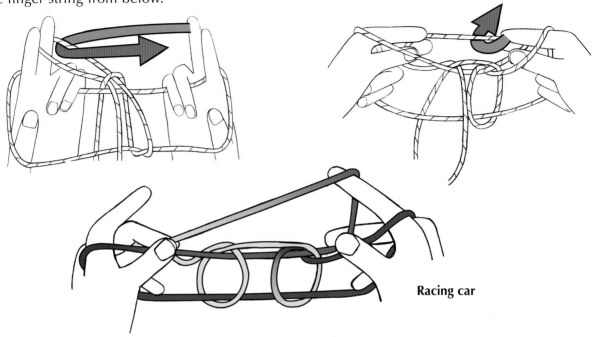

Racing car

10. Change the way the figure is held for 'Too many on the roof' and …

11. 'Too many inside.'

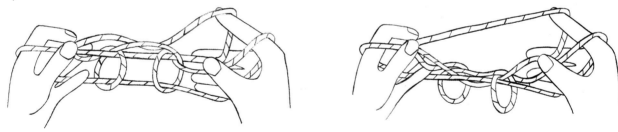

12. Release left middle finger for 'Car driver.' Release top right index for 'Car driver running after car.'

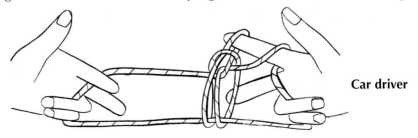

Car driver

Pig and tortoise

Make 'Little fishes' (see page 67). The 'Pig' is formed if the sides of the 'W' are taken (the 'Tortoise' if one side of the 'W' and one entry or exit) by the thumbs followed by all the instructions for the 'Frog' (see page 67).

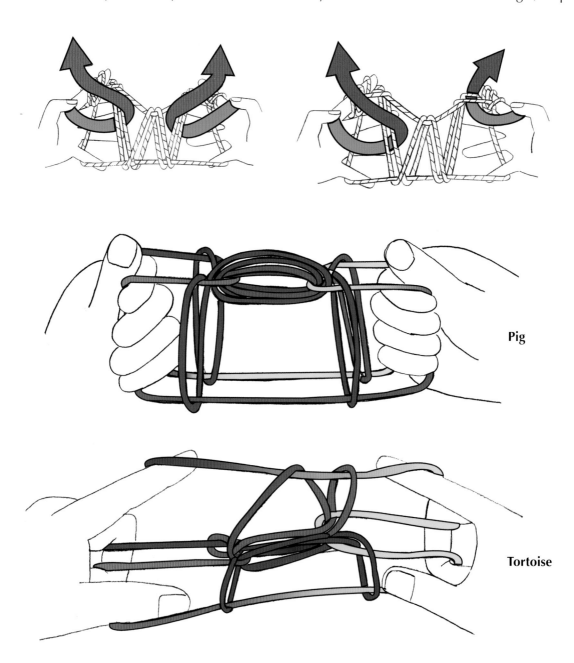

Pig

Tortoise

Moving Figures

Man climbing a tree

1. Make Opening A. Little fingers, over intervening strings, get near thumb string.

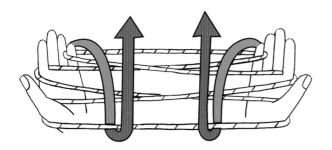

2. Lift lower little finger loops over upper and off the fingers (from the back so they hook palm strings between index and little fingers).

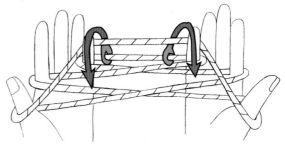

3. Place foot on little finger string. Release little fingers. Index fingers hook palm strings (between index lines). Drop all but hooked strings.

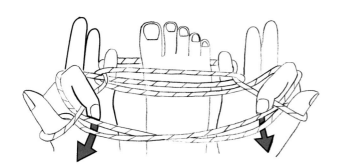

4. Holding just the hooked strings, put tension into the lines leading to the foot and release a little at a time for 'Man climbing a tree.'

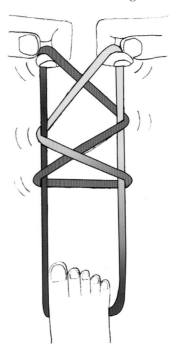

73

Running caribou

1. Make Opening A. Turn right hand, palm away, and close all four fingers over all the strings, but keep thumb upright.

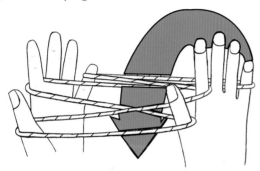

2. Pinch nearest string between index on top and middle finger below.

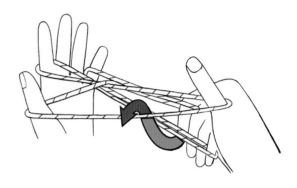

3. Return all four fingers to their original upright position along with the pinched string. Release thumb string.

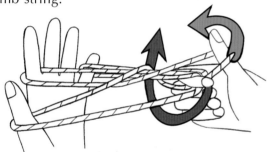

4. Rotate right index around its own strings (away, down and back).

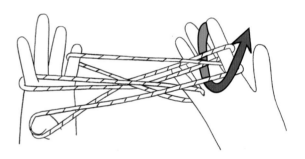

5. Right thumb shares and widens both index loops. Release left thumb string (not shown).

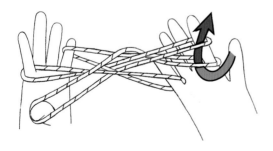

6. Left thumb holds near left index taut. Right thumb pulls far left index string through shared index/thumb loop. Lift this shared loop off index and thumb and drop (not shown).

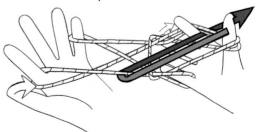

7. Hook right strings with right index (it doesn't really matter where).

8. Release left index ('front leg' dangles). Left index shares right thumb loop and returns (shortening 'front leg').

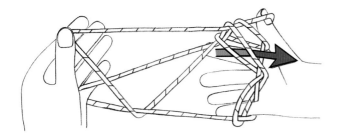

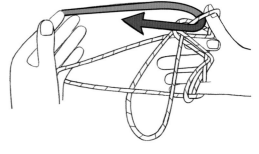

9. Release right thumb and 'head' moves forward.

10. Release right index. Right thumb shares little finger loop (to lift caribou up). Hold left strings to stop caribou running too fast.

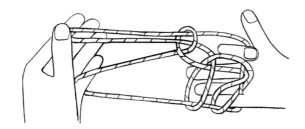

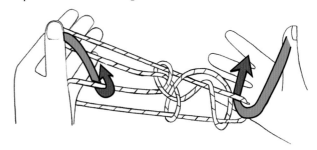

11. Left thumb can lift near little finger string to hold 'rope' around the 'neck.' Pull hands apart to make the 'caribou' run. Release left index to make the caribou disappear.

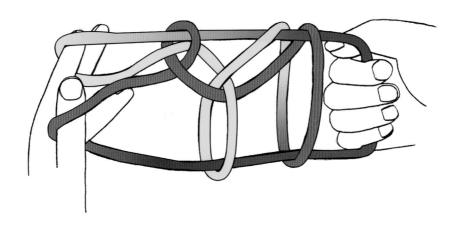

Talking mouth (1)

1. Make Opening A. Thumbs share index loops from near side. Little fingers share from far side.

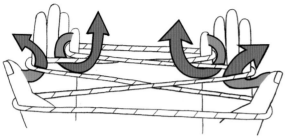

2. Lift lower loops over upper and off their fingers. Release index fingers.

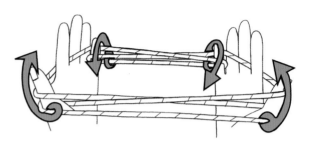

3. Rotate index fingers down into thumb loops and up into little finger loops.

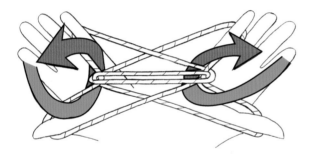

4. Keep index but drop all else. Little, ring and middle fingers enter from below to share index loops.

5. Open and close 'Talking mouth' by rotating hands, thumbs towards then away from each other.

Talking mouth (2)

1&2. Index fingers take palm strings from above. Each time straighten up on return.

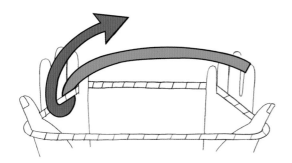 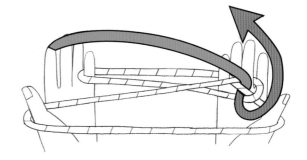

3&4. Thumbs and little fingers take index loops from below and index fingers are released.

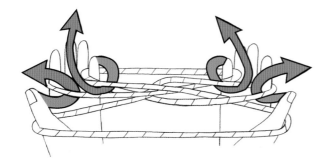

5. Lift off near string connecting thumbs and far string connecting little fingers. This can be done with the teeth or as shown simply by closing fingers to hold cross in place while top and bottom framing stings slip to centre of figure.

6. Follow instructions (3,4&5) of Talking mouth (1).

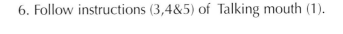

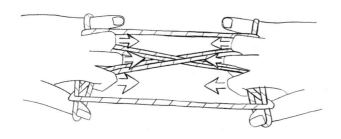 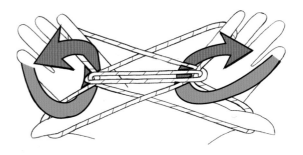

The bat

From The Guianas, South America

1. Place loop over left wrist. Bring both strings in front of left palm and then between index and middle. Near string returns near side of index. Far string returns far side of middle.

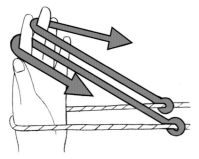

2. Thumb, over other strings, takes far middle string from below.

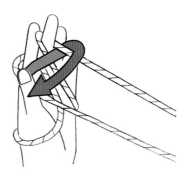

3. Little finger, over other strings, takes far thumb / near index string from below.

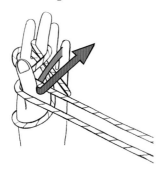

4. Right index takes (from below) the string that links middle finger and thumb. Right middle finger takes (from below) the string that links index and little finger.

5. Lift (with opposite hand) back of hand string over the fingers and drop into the middle.

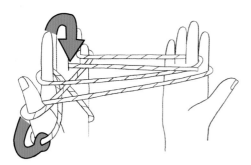

6. By putting right index to left index and right middle to left middle, place right strings on left finger tips.

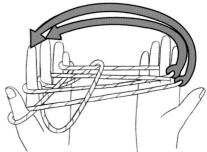

7. Lift lower loops over upper and off the fingers.

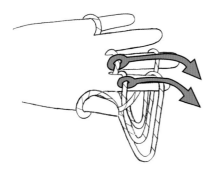

8. Right index removes left index, right middle removes left middle, both from tip side.

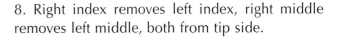
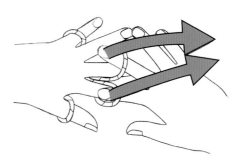

9&10. Display the 'bat' right hand uppermost. To make the 'bat' fly release left hand and pull string out between 'wings,' placing string back on left thumb and little finger.

11. Widen both hands (little fingers away from thumbs) and pull hands apart to make 'bat' fly. Tuck right thumb behind 'bat' and point with right index and outstretched arm into the distance as it disappears.

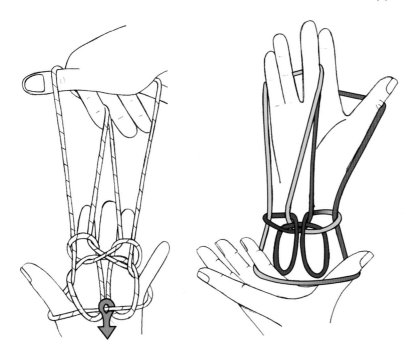
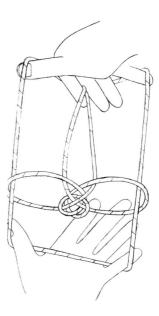

Two fish swimming away

1&2. Place loop on thumbs and little fingers. Whole hands (even thumbs) enter palm strings from below.

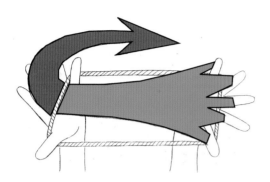 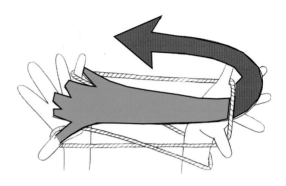

3. Index fingers enter little finger loops from above, then thumb loops from above, then straighten up through the middle collecting the far thumb string.

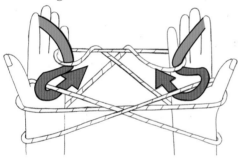

4. Release thumbs ('Cat's face' appears if held loosely). Thumbs take index loops from below. Release index fingers.

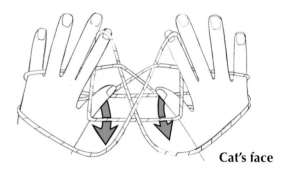

Cat's face

5. Place wrist strings on thumbs and little fingers.

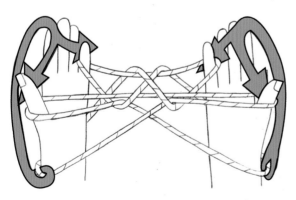

6. Index fingers enter little finger loop, then thumb loops from above, then straighten up through the middle (collecting far thumb string). Release little fingers.

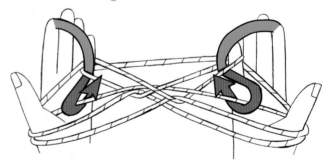

7. Pass index loops to little fingers. Release index fingers.

8. Hold hands out so that a 'Boat with two masts' appears. Index fingers hook up central horizontal string on either side of the 'two masts.'

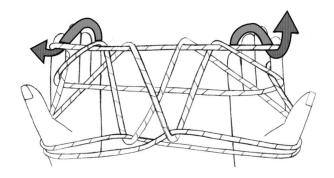

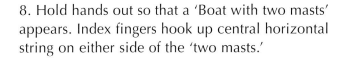

Boat with two masts

9&10. Slowly release thumbs from both their loops.

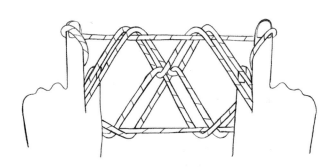

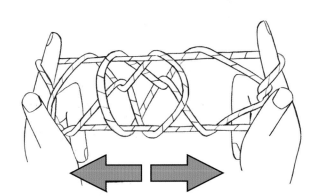

11. Pull hands apart to make the 'Two fish' swim away.

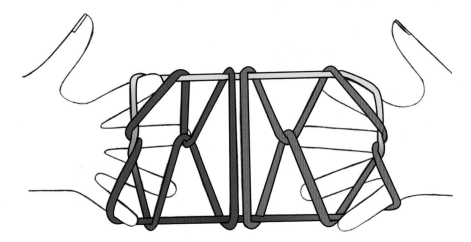

Well, Sunflower and Two Men

1. Make Opening A. Index fingers rotate down into little finger loops and up between own strings and thumb strings. Drop little finger strings.

2. Little fingers, ring fingers and middle fingers hook down index loops from far side.

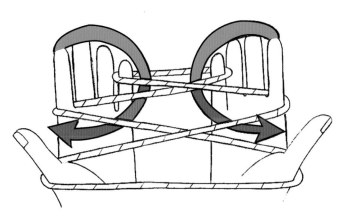

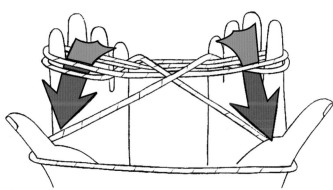

3. Middle fingers still hooked, stretch out to take thumb loops from below so that thumbs can be released.

4. Thumbs enter middle of figure as shown. Release middle fingers. (Form the 'Well' by instead taking strings marked by blue arrows).

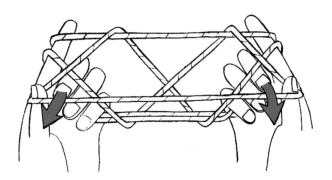

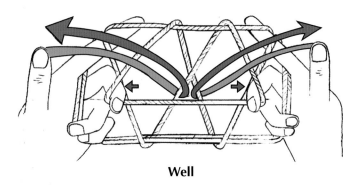

Well

5. Thumbs enter and share upper index loops.

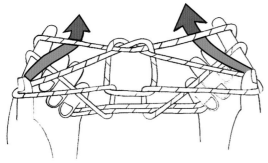

6. Release index fingers from all their loops. Lift off lower thumb loops from the front (left side arrow of drawing shows left index removing loop).

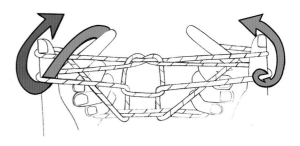

7. Index fingers take thumb loops from far side. Release thumbs.

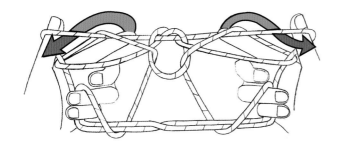

8. Thumbs enter hooked loops from tip side and pull them to the side of the palm strings.

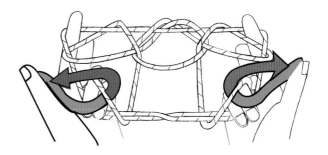

9. Thumbs lift palm strings through hooked loops. Release hooked fingers.

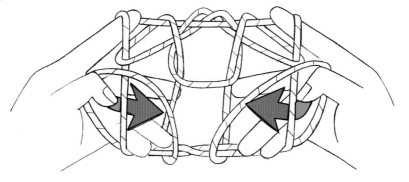

10. Pass right index to left, right thumb to left (both tip-to-tip).

11. Right index tip-to-tip takes index loops, right middle, ring and little take thumb loops.

12. Left thumb and little finger take right index strings. Re-arrange 'Sunflower' as necessary.

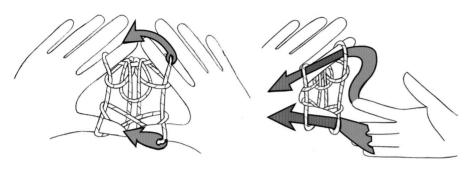

13&14. Pull 'head' down (with right hand) and stretch away to make flower grow. Drawing shows index seeming to drip water.

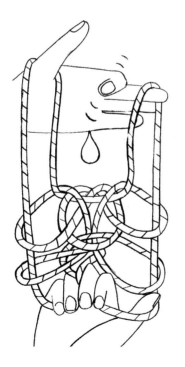

Sunflower

15. Place on edge to show 'Two men' (one with a big belly).

16. Let go of left index and place left index with lower fingers. Raise right index to help men remain tall.

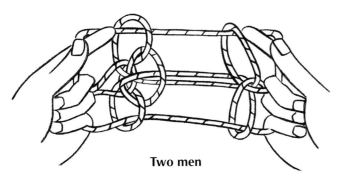

Two men

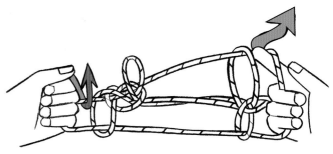

17. Move hands apart to make one man walk from left to right.

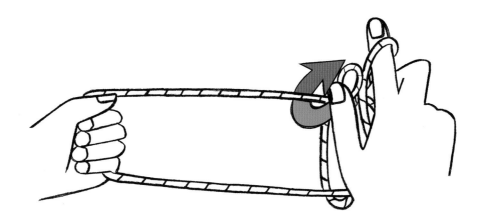

Other Figures

Japanese butterfly

1. Place on thumbs and left little finger. Right little finger takes left palm string from above.

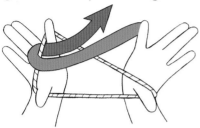

2. Index fingers take near little finger string from below.

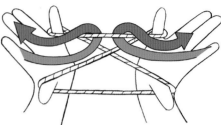

3&4. Middle fingers takes palm strings from below on both sides.

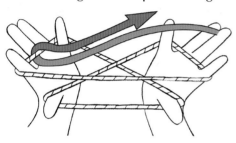

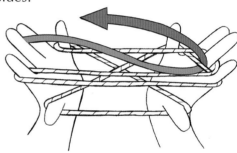

5. Little fingers over intervening strings take far thumb strings.

6. Index fingers rotate down into own loops (over palm strings) and up under thumbs strings. Drop thumbs.

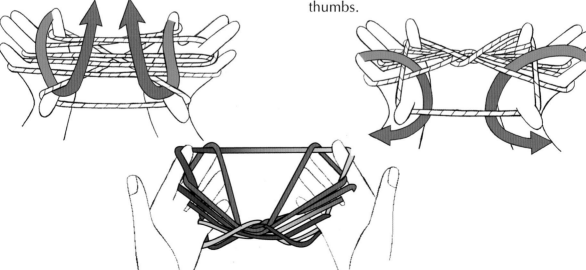

Ringing bell

1. Make Japanese Butterfly. Index fingers move away through large triangles in 'wings' (losing own loops in the process).

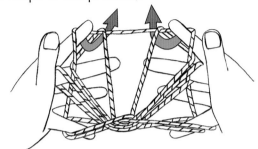

2. Little fingers rotate towards centre of figure around their own loops.

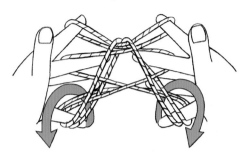

3. Pinch 'little finger twists' with ring fingers and thumbs. Release little fingers. Carefully release pinched knots so that the 'Bell' form appears. This form requires quite a stiff string.

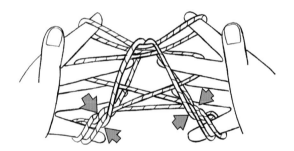

4. Hold bell as shown below and move from side to side so that outer shell strikes interior and 'bell rings.'

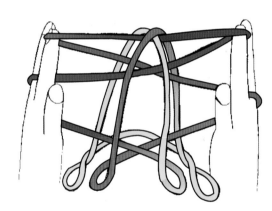

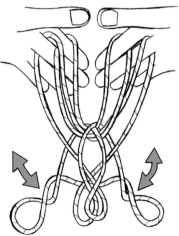

Lightning flash

A Navaho action figure (best with a long string)

> This is a storm cloud, changing shape.
> People are running
> To escape the thunder and lightning ... FLASH!

1. Hold loop 'storm cloud' and make a twist in the top, placing index fingers in the top part of the resulting figure of eight and thumbs in the lower part as shown. Thumbs lift lower part of loop and hands spread apart as shown.

2. Thumbs enter index loops from above to take far index strings.

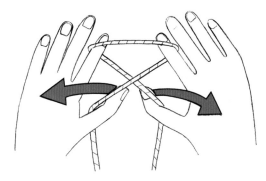

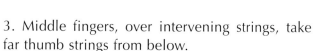

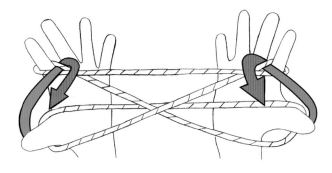

3. Middle fingers, over intervening strings, take far thumb strings from below.

4. Ring fingers take middle/palm strings from below.

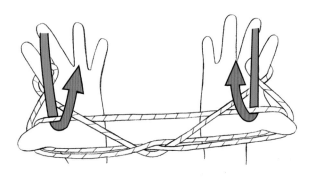

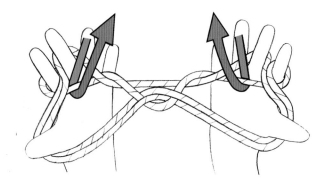

5. Little fingers take ring/palm strings from below.

6. Separate little finger strings (while keeping loops around the fingers tight — by fingers squeezing together — and while throwing double thumb strings over back strings so they spread out better) by pushing near little finger strings downwards with thumbs for 'Lightning flash.'

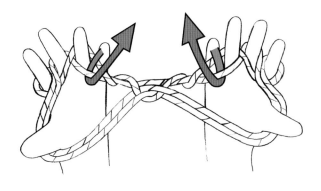

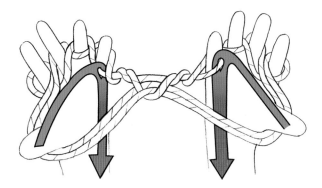

7. A shorter 'Flash' can be made by missing out 4&5.

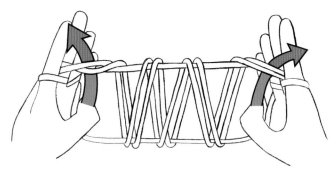

8. Thumbs re-take double strings at top of figure to repeat stage 6 and make another 'Lightning flash.'

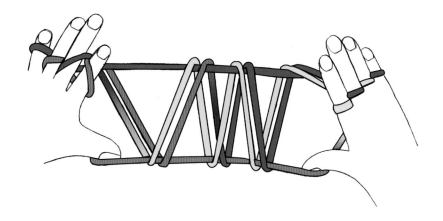

The rabbit

1. Make Opening A. Index fingers take near thumb string from above (middle fingers help by temporarily squeezing from below), then below near thumb string and away above all other strings, thus giving the index an upper loop. Release thumbs.

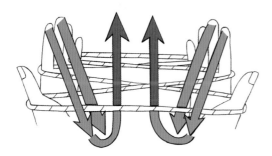

2. Thumbs take furthest string in the following way: Thumbs first go under index loops to enter little finger loops from below. Then they continue finger-tip-side of all strings except upper near index string which they hook back the way they came below far little finger string which is lifted by the thumbs.

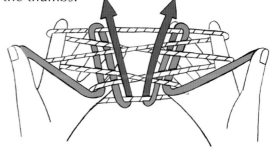

3. Thumbs remove top index loop from below and take that loop back through own loop which is dropped.

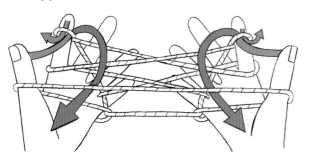

4. Release little fingers and close middle, ring and little fingers over all strings except near thumb string.

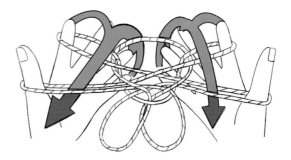

5. Lift thumbs high to pull the 'Ears' out of the 'Rabbit.' Index fingers can help form figure from far side.

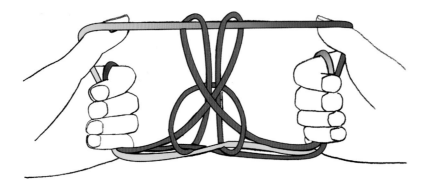

Olympic flag

1. Place loop on little fingers. Left index takes near left little finger string from above, pointing towards yourself as it returns.

2. Right index takes left palm string from above (on the far side of the far left index string), pointing away from yourself as it returns.

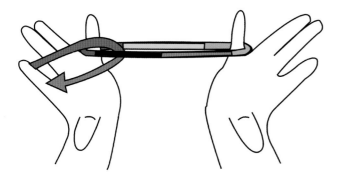

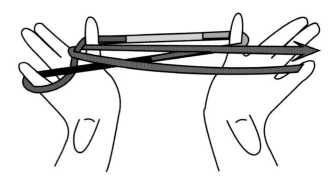

3. Thumbs go over near index strings, under far index and under near little finger strings. Thumbs return with near little finger strings the way they came. Release index loops now (not shown).

4. Pull near thumb strings to make the **First Olympic Ring** smaller.

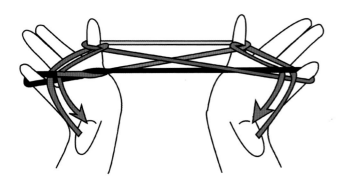

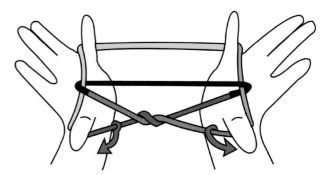

5. Take the left little finger loop completely off the little finger, bring it **down** through thumb loop and place it **below** far thumb string.

The right hand should do this as shown in the next picture.

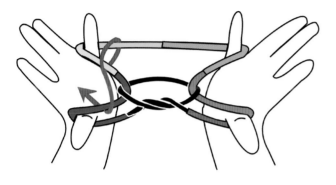

6. Pull the blue string **down** through the loop and place it on the left little finger.

(The picture shows the little finger achieving this is one movement.) Open hands to reveal **2nd Circle**.

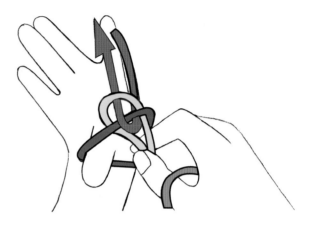

7. Take the right little finger loop completely off the little finger, bring it **up** through the thumb loop and place it **on top of** the far thumb string.

The left hand should do this as shown in the next picture.

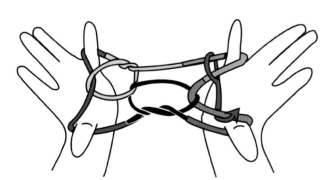

8. Pull the red string **up** through the loop and place it on the right little finger. (The picture shows the little finger achieving this in one movement.) **3rd Circle**.

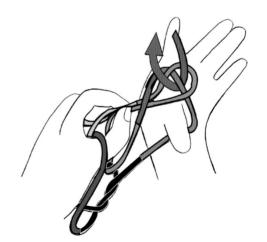

9. Pull the left near little finger string **up** through the left thumb loop and **over** the near thumb string.

(The right hand can do this by entering the left thumb loop from **above** to get the string and then pulling it over.)

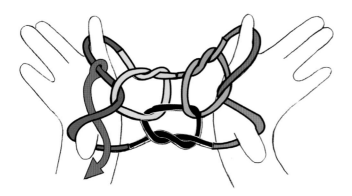

10. Pull the near thumb string **up** through the loop that has just been pulled over and place this string on the left thumb once that thumb has dropped its own loop. Open hands for **4th Circle.**

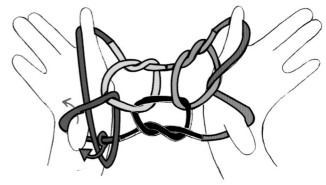

11. Pull the right near little finger string **down** through the right thumb loop and **under** the near thumb string. (The left hand can do this by entering the right thumb loop from **below** to get the string and then pulling it over.)

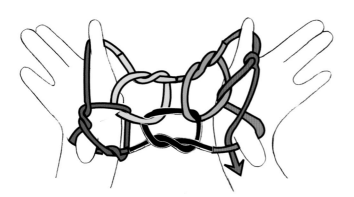

12. Pull the near right thumb string **down** through the held loop and place on the right thumb once that thumb has dropped its own loop. (The arrow shows the right thumb doing this in one movement.) Open hands for **5th Circle.**

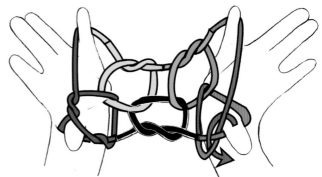

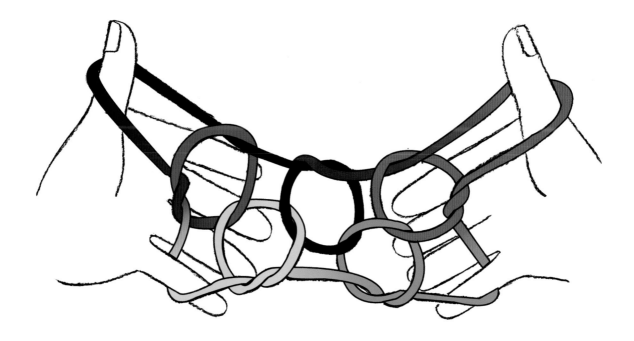

Traditionally the five circles represent the five continents of the world, and the five colours (plus the white of the background) are the colours present in the flags of the world.

Old-fashioned telephone

1. Make 'Opening A' with a short or doubled string. Rotate index fingers by moving them down into the little finger loops, under index strings and up between near index and far thumb strings. Release little fingers.

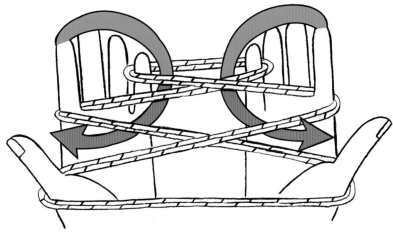

2. Shake index fingertips as the 'Telephone' rings. Release left thumb and then left index. Now you have the 'Handset' in your right hand put it next to your ear and speak into what was the double left index loop to answer the phone call.

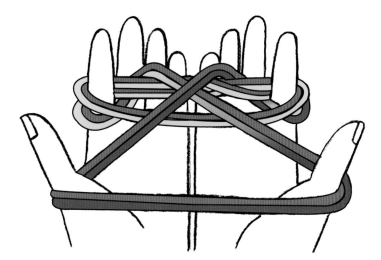

The Porcupine

A Navaho and Inuit Figure called the 'Porcupine' by the Navajo, and 'Wolverine' or 'Arctic Fox' by the Inuit.

1. Make Opening A (and then swap index loops so that they 'hook' together in the middle in the following way ...) Left index takes right index loop off from tip side and holds it on the tip of the left index.

2. Right index takes lower (original) left index loop off from the tip side (and over the tip index loop).

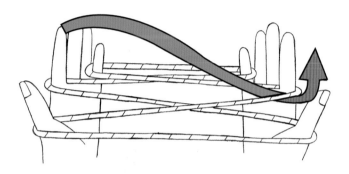

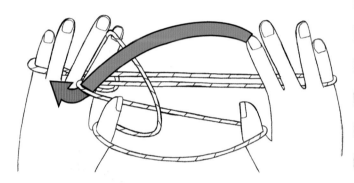

3. Left thumb takes off left index and little finger loops from the base.

4. Left little finger goes up through the lower two thumb loops, hooks the top far thumb string from the far side and returns down through all the thumb loops with the hooked string.

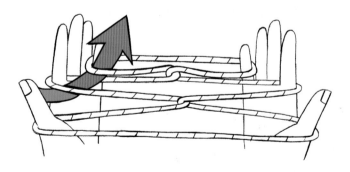

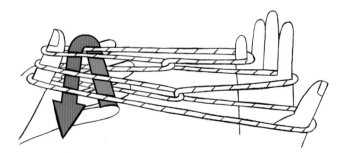

5. Left index goes down through the thumb loops, the near side of the lowest near thumb string and returns through all the thumb loops with the string. Release left thumb strings.

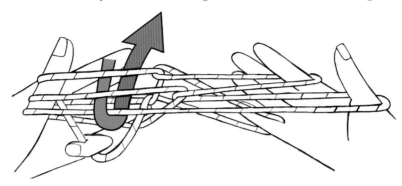

6. Left thumb takes double central strings (just above lowest string) and then removes left index string from below.

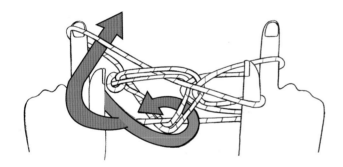

7. Opposite hand lifts lower (double) strings over upper and off the thumb.

8. Release all right strings except index . Hold index string with four fingers to display the 'Porcupine.' Pull figure to the right and it can be made to run to the left. Flick top right string to make the 'tail' twitch.

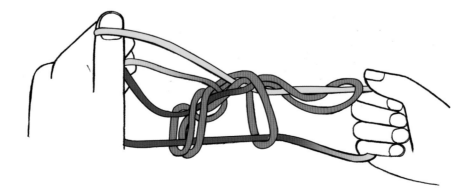

Partner Games

Sawing

1. Make Opening A.

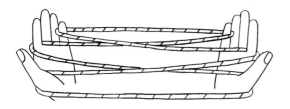

2. Now a second player makes Opening A from the side.

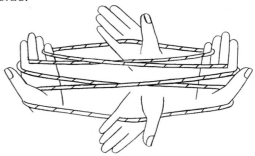

3-6. Both players keep index loops but drop everything else and start 'Sawing.'

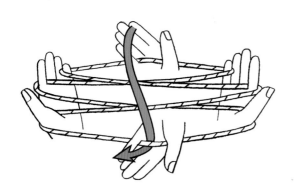

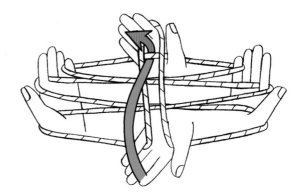

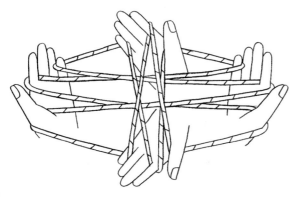

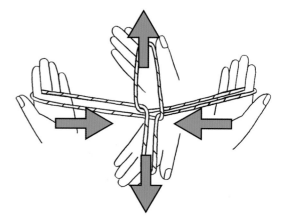

Cutting the hand

1. Make Opening A.

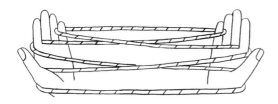

2. A friend puts a hand DOWN through the middle.

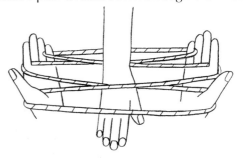

3,4&5. Keep thumbs but drop everything else. Make Opening A again in the SAME ORDER.

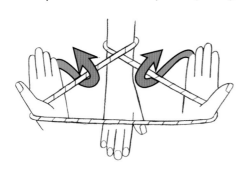

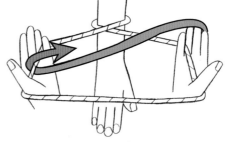

6. Trapped hand goes UP through the middle.

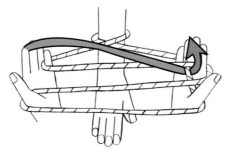

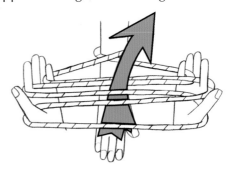

7&8 Keep thumbs but drop everything else and hand is freed!

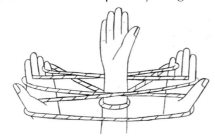

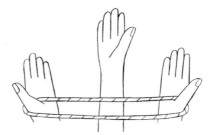

Cat's-cradle

1. Place loop around palms. Wrap near string near around palms.

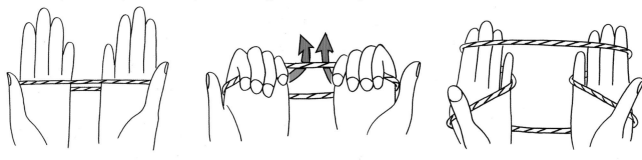

2. Right middle takes left palm from below. Repeat on other side in centre to make 'Cradle'.

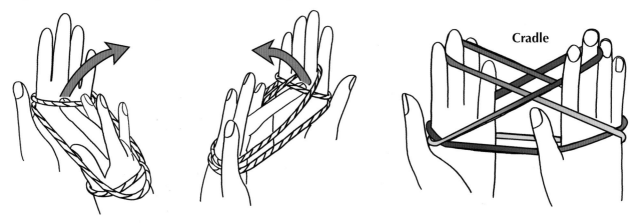

Cradle

3. Second player pulls pinched crosses over and back under framing strings, lifts off and opens to make 'Soldier's bed.'

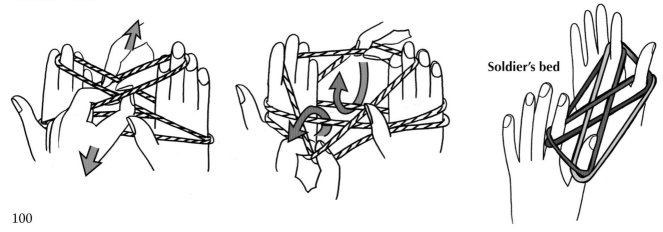

Soldier's bed

4. First player pulls pinched crosses over and back under framing strings, lifts off and opens to make 'Candles.'

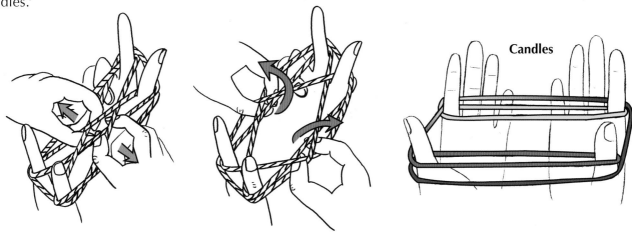

Candles

5. Hook far 'candle' string with upturned little finger and pull to side. Repeat on other side. Thumbs and index lift framing strings and open for 'Manger.'

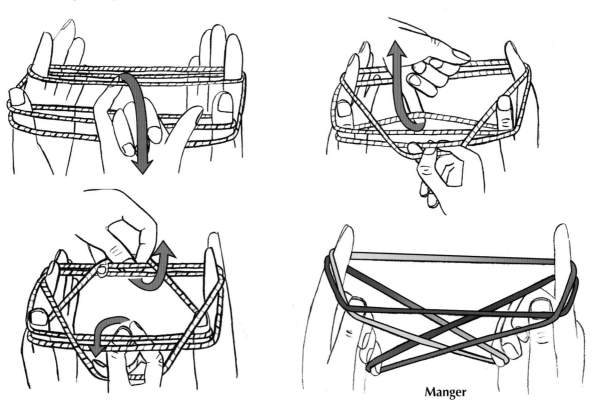

Manger

6. Pinch crosses, pull out over framing strings and pointing downwards remove for 'Diamonds.'

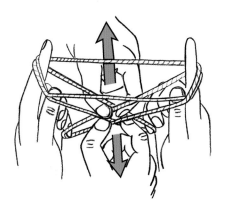 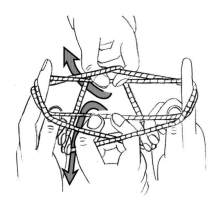 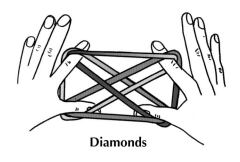

Diamonds

7. Pinch crosses, pull out over framing strings and back up for 'Cat's-eye.'

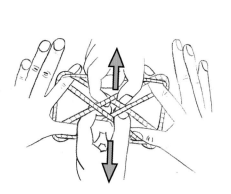 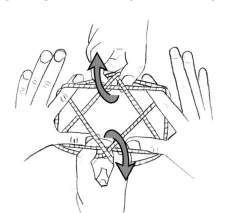 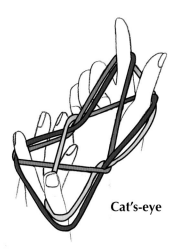

Cat's-eye

8. Pinch sides of 'eye.' Turn upwards and lift off for 'Fish on the dish.' Hook central strings with little fingers.

 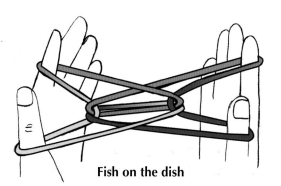 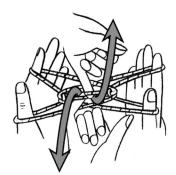

Fish on the dish

9. Pull out, pinch crosses in framing strings, turn upwards and lift off for 'Hand Drum.'

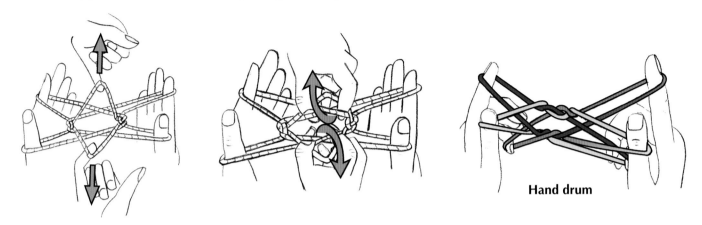

Hand drum

10. Pinch little finger strings together, pull out to reveal frame, turn up through triangles then down over frame. Point down and take off for 'Diamonds' again.

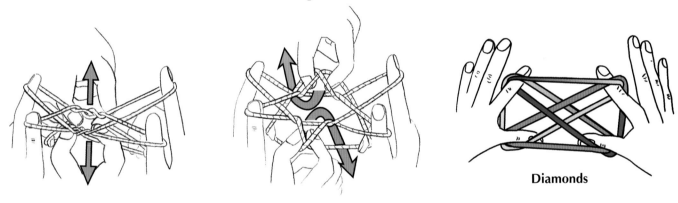

Diamonds

Other ways to continue Cat's-cradle:

Cradle to Sawing
Second player takes framing strings, first keeps middle fingers only to 'saw' (See 'Sawing' page 98).
Cat's-eye to Manger
Second player's little fingers take outermost edges of 'eye' while thumbs and index fingers take off central strings for 'manger.'
Opening 'A' to Manger
Second player's little fingers take opposite framing strings, crossing them as during 'Candles-to-Manger,' and thumbs and index fingers enter centre to take off for 'Manger.'

Tortoise shell

(Can be made on a friend's hands)
1. Place loop on index and ring fingers.

2. Middle finger takes short palm string. Repeat on other side as in Opening A.

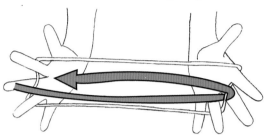 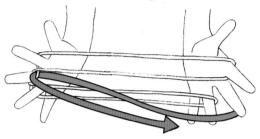

3-7. Choose one of the middle/ring strings. Take it below the lowest string and up over the next. One by one lift each straight string through to catch the previous.

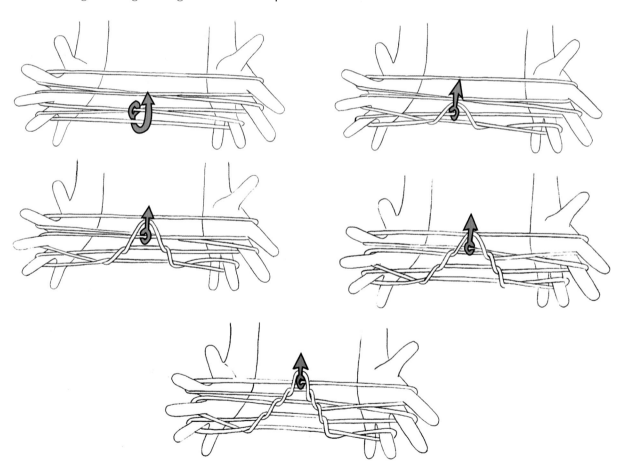

8. Place the top string onto both thumbs.

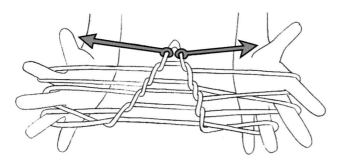

9&10. Repeat the pattern downwards (and up and down again). Place the last string over both little fingers.

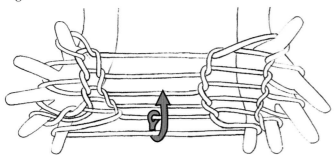
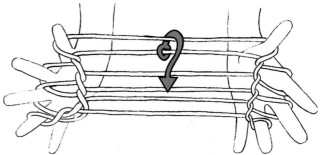

11&12. Close hands then open, splaying fingers as shown.

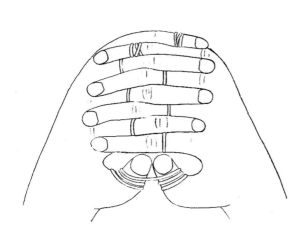
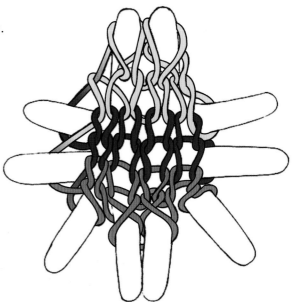

Tricks

Free or caught

1. Make Opening A and release right index.

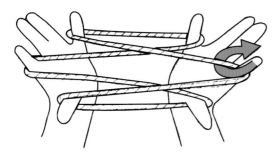

2. Left index hooks palm string through its own loop while dropping all other left strings for the 'Sword.'

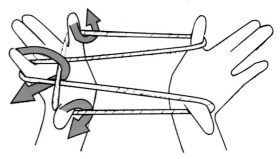

3. Put index string on thumb and little finger.

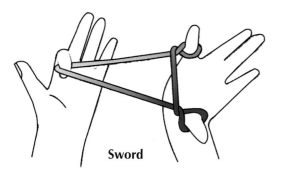

Sword

4. Left index goes down into right palm string, straightens up and returns.

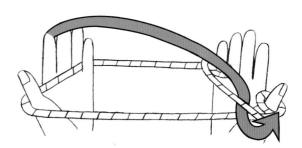

5&6. Right index points down into right thumb loop and pulls far thumb string over little finger loop, then goes down into little finger loop and straightens up towards the middle.

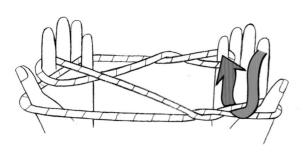

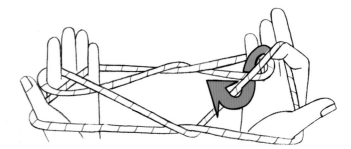

7. Right little finger hooks down extension of far thumb string through index and thumb loops. Left little finger hooks down far index through thumb loop.

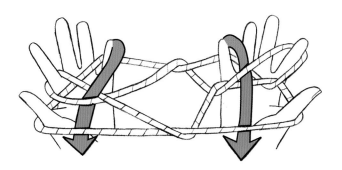

8. Release thumbs. Hold out 'Three diamonds.' Press in sides with pinched thumbs and middle fingers if they are too squashed.

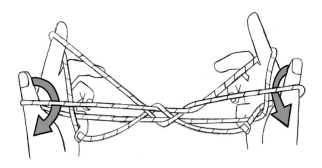

9. Ask someone to place a hand through the centre. Let go of left hand and right index and pull to the right and hand is trapped. Or let go of right hand and left index and pull to the left and hand is freed.

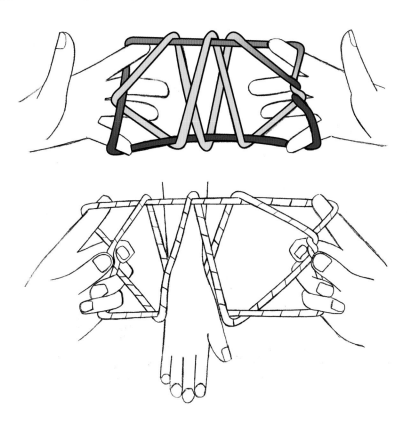

The lizard

Hang loop on left wrist. Move right hand into loop from tip side, Point down, circle around whole loop and return through loop from forearm side. As right hand leaves loop, palms face each other. The whole move can be smooth and simple but if not correct then hand gets caught!

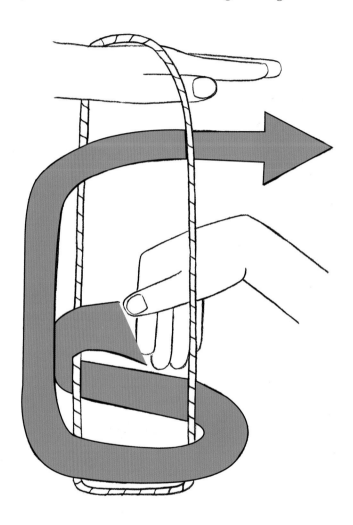

Early Hawaiians would win bets from passing strangers with this string trick. Though sure they could do it, after seeing it once, strangers usually ended up with their hands caught rather than free.

Wandering loop

1&2. Hang loop on middle finger. Wrap both strings over index so that the short index string is on the palm side and the shared middle and index string is tip side. Continue winding string around middle and index. (It doesn't matter how many times you wind the loops but they must be kept tidy).

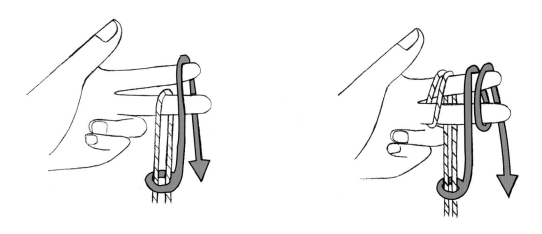

3&4. Let fall (or push off) the furthest tip side string. Unwind and the loop is on the index!

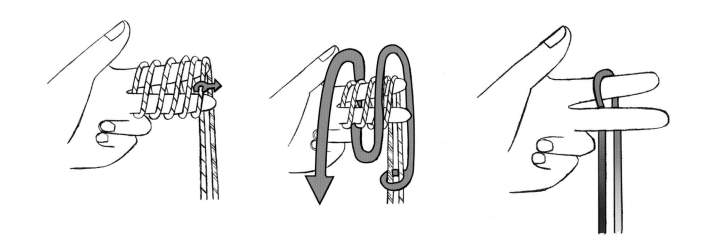

Thumb jump

1&2. Make Opening A.

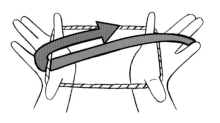
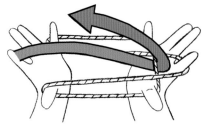

3. Index fingers lift off thumb loops from tip side.

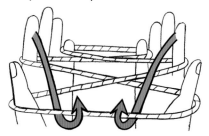

4&5. Index fingers rotate three times around their own double loops, away then up. Release little fingers but don't pull hands apart. Little, ring and middle fingers take index loops from below and close as in a fist. Release index.

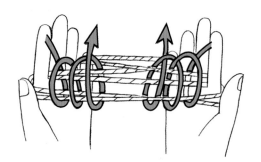
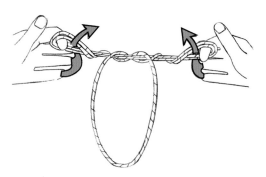

6&7. Index and thumbs enter loops from tip side, move towards centre then spread apart, unwinding loops which can jump onto a friend's thumb.

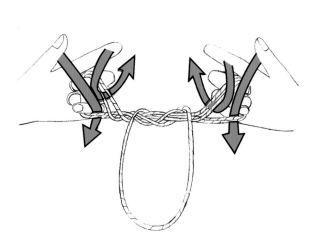
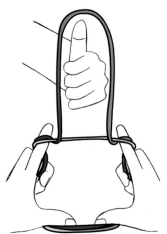

Through thumb

1. Place one end of the loop on someone's thumb and the other hooked on your right index.

2. Place your left thumb down into the centre of the loop and lift the right string over the left by turning your left index in an anticlockwise arc.

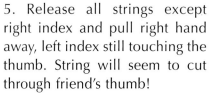

3. Stretch left hand down and swing right hand to the right. Hook where strings cross with right middle finger.

4. Pull right hand back and touch friend's thumb tip with left index tip.

5. Release all strings except right index and pull right hand away, left index still touching the thumb. String will seem to cut through friend's thumb!

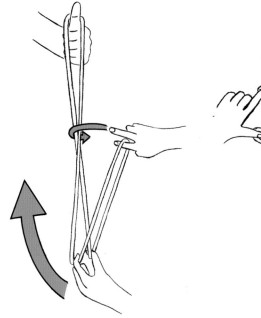

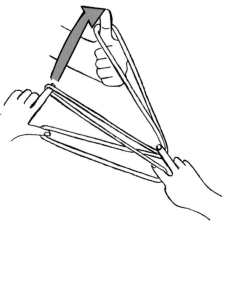

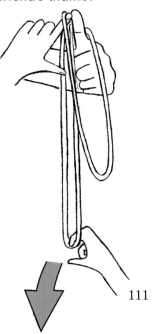

111

One hand knot

Use an untied one-metre (3 feet) length of string or use your loop as a single string

1. Hang string on right palm. One strand passes between little finger and ring finger. Turn palm down. Use index and middle fingers to pinch other string.

2. Allow the string that passes over the back of the hand to fall over this pinched string. (Release little finger too).

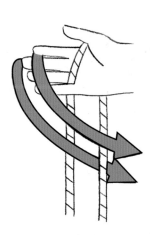

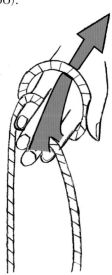

3. Holding just the pinched string turn hand (or use thumb) to pull the bow out of the knot. (Don't make this string too long). The whole movement should be smooth and quick.

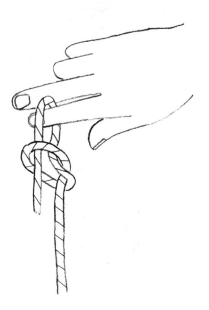

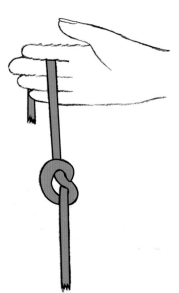

Smith's secret (sometimes called 'Fool's Knot')

1. Hang loop on left palm.

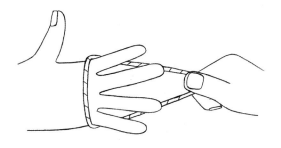

2. Bring index string back between index and middle fingers and bring little finger string back between little finger and ring finger. Wrap both strings around left thumb.

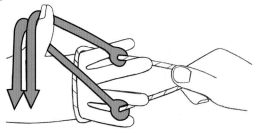

3. Take strings back the way they came.

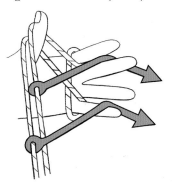

4. Allow little finger string to drop while index string is brought around the index and laid on the palm.

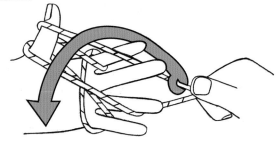

5. Take thumb loops off thumb and place them between middle finger and ring finger.

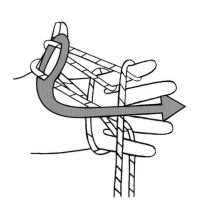

6. Remove in one go by pulling palm string.

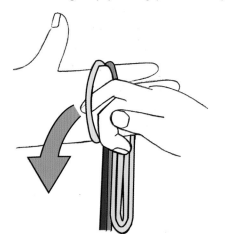

Thrown knot

Use a one-metre (3 feet) length of string with a small weight tied to one end — perhaps a nut from your tool box

1&2. Lay the weighted end (nut) on the floor and practise 'throwing' a wave down towards it.

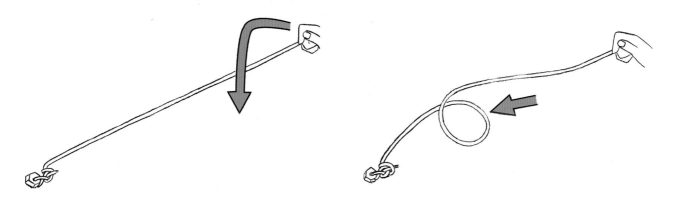

3,4&5. Start swinging the rope as a pendulum. As the nut reaches its height throw the wave so that the nut falls through the loop (or the loop wraps over the nut).

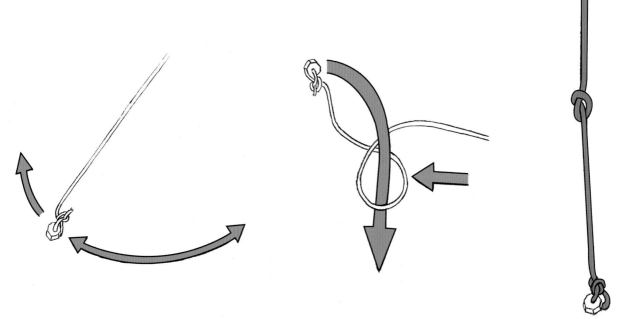

Indian rope trick

Use a one-metre (3 feet) length of string

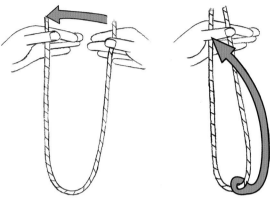

1&2. Display your length of string. Announce that you are going to cut it in half. Pass right-hand string to left, then lift the half way point (the lowest point) up to the left hand.

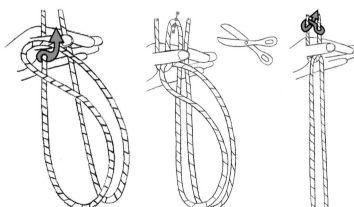

3,4&5. Place the half way point on one of the strings in your left palm. In one smooth movement pick up this string instead and put it ready for cutting. Cut.
(The trick can finish now by pulling out the rope revealing that it wasn't cut after all — though a small portion is hidden in your left hand!)

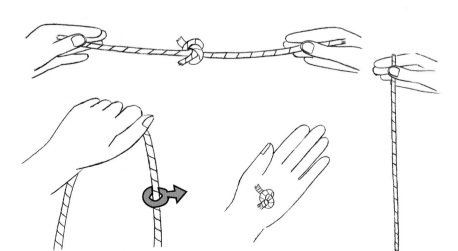

6–9. Release two of your four strings so that you appear to be holding two equal cut lengths (a 'link' is hidden behind thumb). Tie the exposed tops. Hold out your string. Grab the knot and it can be made to slide off revealing the string made whole again!

St Lawrence knot trick

1&2. Hold loop in palms. Turn right hand swiftly over (as if checking wristwatch) to send a wave onto out-stretched left index. Index enters wave so that a complete index loop is created. (Place it on if you prefer!)

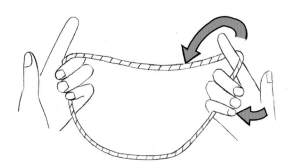
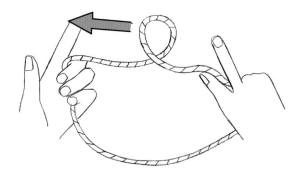

3,4&5. Throw two or three more waves (figure a). Left thumb pushes index string against tip of left index while right hand pushes index loops off onto this string (figure b), which is then placed on the left index, having gone through the three loops (figure c).

a

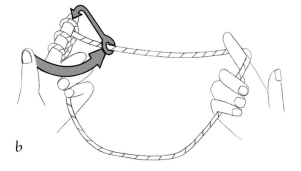

b

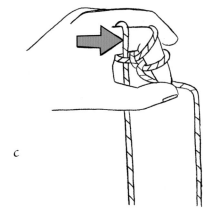

c

6. Hold the tangle in the right fist and then slowly pull away revealing the knots as they form (beautifully spaced).

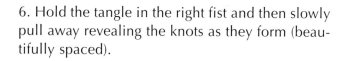

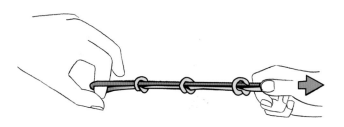

Cutting the body

1. Place loop around body. Hold ends with thumbs.

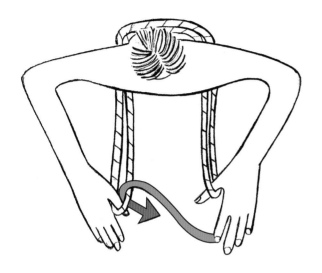

2. Share one thumb loop with the opposite index. Widen this loop.

3. Keep widening loop and drop other thumb loop.

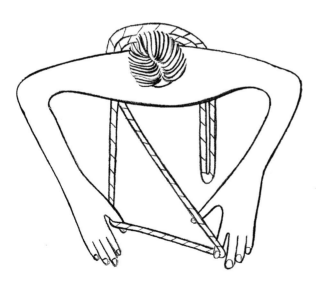

4. String is now in front!

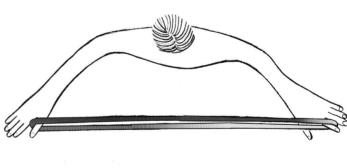

String Things

Monkey chain and scoubidou

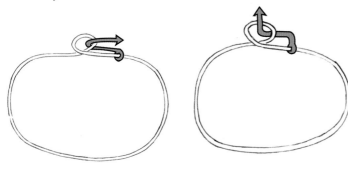

1. Make a small loop. Put upper near portion under and through to make new small loop.

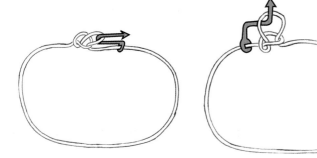

2. Repeat each time on the same side for the 'Monkey chain' and on alternate sides to make the 'Scoubidou.'

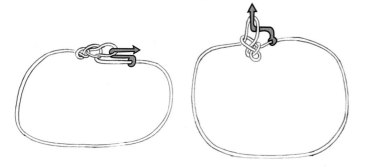

3. Tighten growing 'scoubidou' by pulling the string which is pushed through the small loop before it goes through.

Scoubidou man

1. Make a 'scoubidou' ten segments long. Repeat on opposite side of string loop.

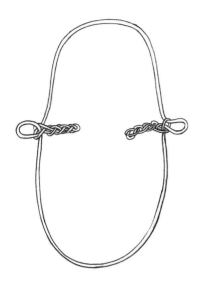

2. Place the small loops together and treat as one. Put near portion of a double side string through to make a new small loop and make a 'scoubidou' four segments long treating long double loops as one.

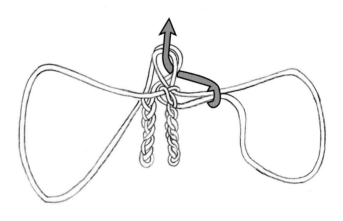

3. Make a small loop in arm near body. Repeat, making 'scoubidou' segments until arm is formed. Place end of arm through last loop as a 'hand.'

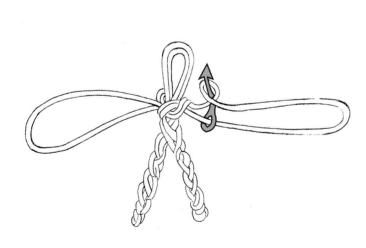

4. Repeat with other arm for the 'String Scoubidou Man.'

Wrist watch

1. Place doubled (or short) string on thumbs and little fingers in basic position. Wrap near strings around little fingers and thumbs (opposite hands can do this).

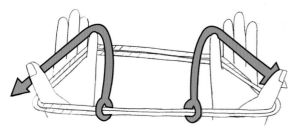

2. Right index takes left palm string.

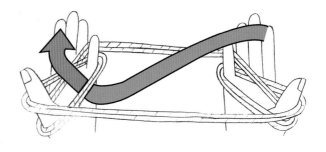

3. Left index takes right palm string.

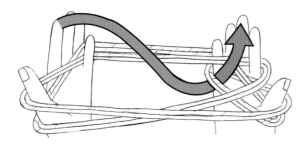

4. Little fingers and thumbs dive down over index stings into the centre of the figure, then straighten up by stretching away from each other.

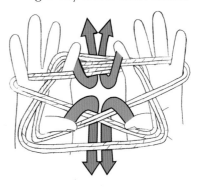

5. Little fingers and thumbs enter index loops from below.

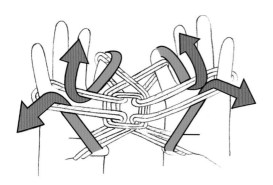

6. Release index. Lift lower loops over upper and off fingers.

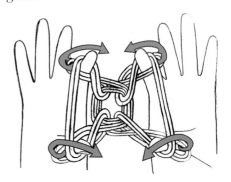

7&8. Take figure off hand. Pull one side pair through the other. Now you have a 'Wrist watch.'

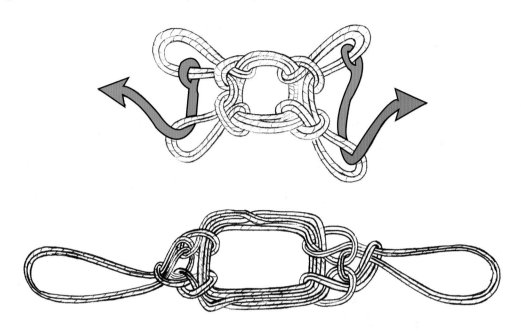

9&10. Over-lap straps. Pull top strap through lower, then tuck as shown, depending on how much remains.

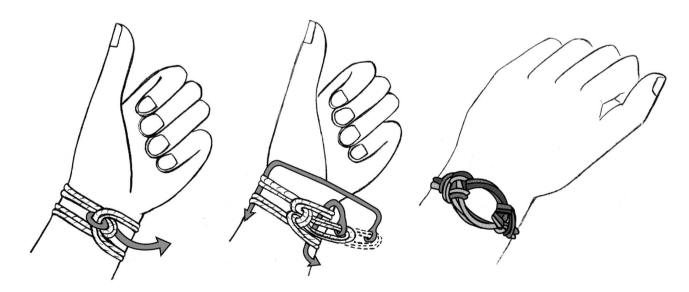

Bolivian footprint

1. Place short or doubled loop on thumbs and little fingers. Left index takes right, hooking down and turning away as it returns.

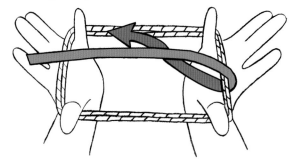

2. Right ring and index fingers take left palm string on either side of the twisted index loop.

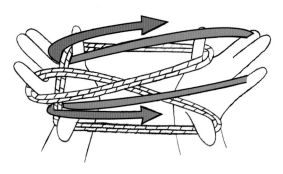

3. Right thumb and little finger enter left index loop from below.

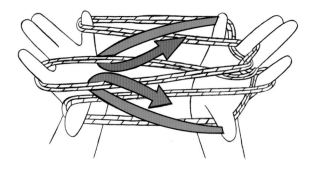

4. Right thumb and little finger then go down into left thumb and little finger loops (thus dropping their lower loops). Drop left thumb and little finger.

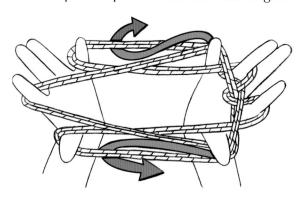

5&6. Lay the 'Bolivian footprint' on the ground, arranging as needed.

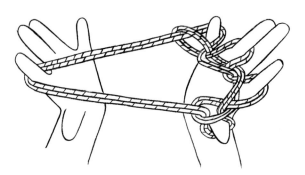

Whizzer

Pass ends of a 50 cm (20 in) length of very thin string ('Friendship Bracelet' cotton or any strong 'thread') through two opposite holes of a button. Tie to form a loop. Throw the button round to get it moving. As it unwinds pull outwards to help it on its way. As it winds release to allow it to turn further. Each time it changes direction pull outwards, then release.

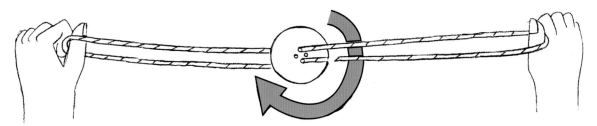

Make your own card whizzer

Cut out a 5 cm (2 in) card circle with one central hole (big enough to easily pass thin string). Pass the middle of the string a short way through the hole. Twist 2½ cm (1 in) of sellotape (shape like a match with a twist in the middle) and place on hole separating the two strands of string, Use further sellotape to attach this 'twist' to the card. Tie the free ends of the string to make a loop. Decorate card with coloured spots (stickers).

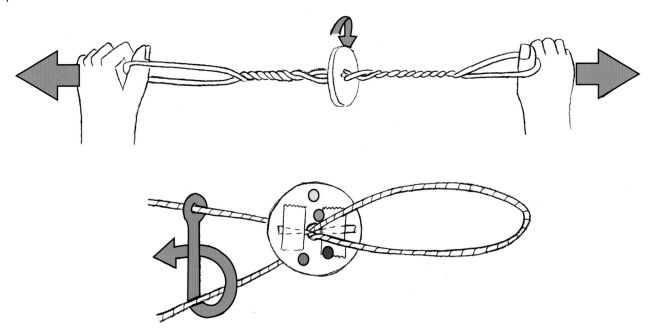

123

Childrens' inventions

Trampoline

1. Place loop on thumbs. Rotate right thumb.

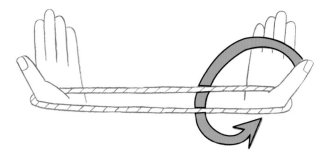

2. Little fingers enter thumb loops from below.

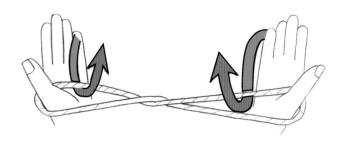

3. Right index takes left palm string from below.

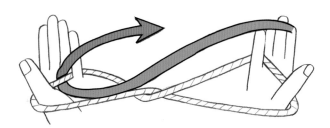

4. Left index takes right palm string from below in middle.

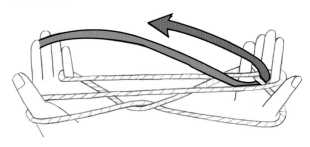

5. 'Twist' hands, (palms up, palms down, palms up, palms down) to make the 'Trampoline' bounce.

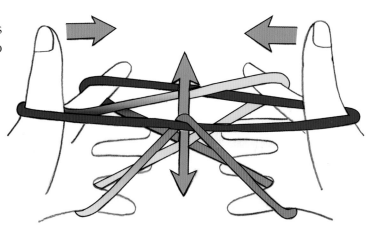

Trampoline to kite

Make the 'Trampoline.' Lift top cross (formed by near index strings) with teeth and drop all strings except little finger strings to form the 'Kite.'

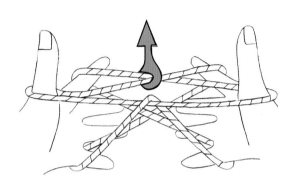 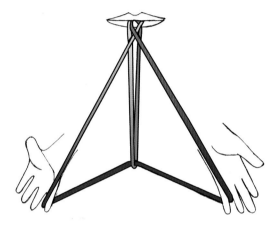

Trampoline to camera

Make the 'Trampoline.' Put index and little finger loops on thumbs. Other fingers enter triple thumb loops from tip side. Thumbs move apart, then together to 'take photos' with the 'Camera.'

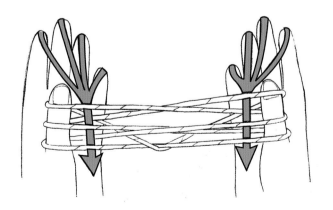 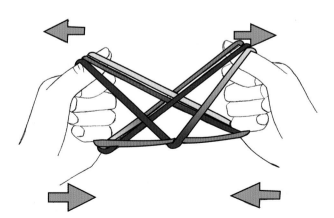

Glove

Lay single strand of string loop so it is woven in and out between the fingers. Wind the single strand until all the string is used up for the 'Glove.'

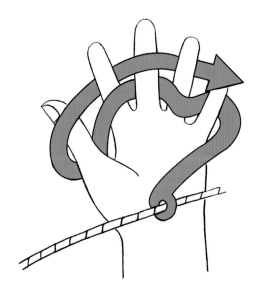 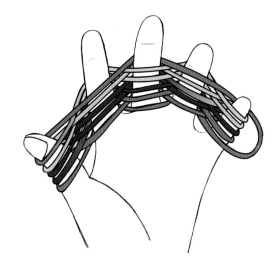

Beard

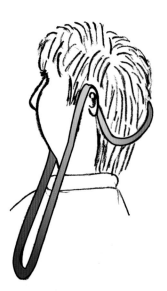

Moat

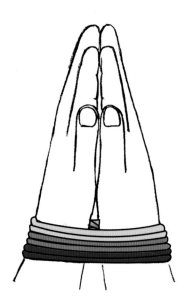

Very Simple Figures

Book

This book opens from above …

1&2. Hold loop as shown. Pull hands apart and together.

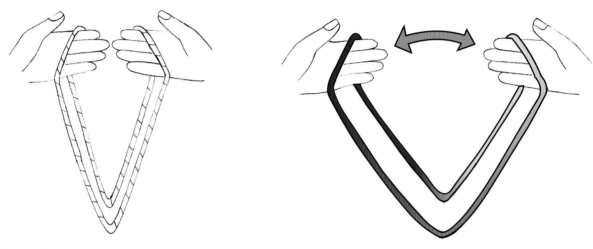

… and from below!

3&4. Pass right hand string to left. Lift one of the two hanging loops to 'open the book from below.'

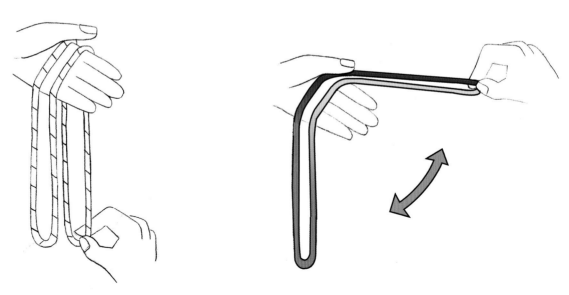

Dewdrops

1. Index fingers hold string. Place right string OVER left string onto left index.

2. Place tip string over base string.

3. Remove new tip string with right hand.

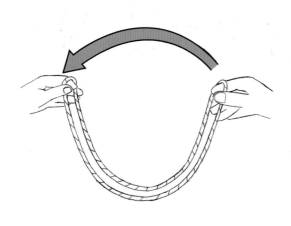

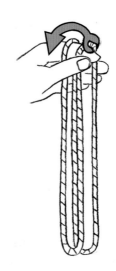

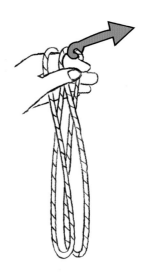

4. Gradually pull apart for 'Dewdrops' to form. Keep moving apart and they disappear.

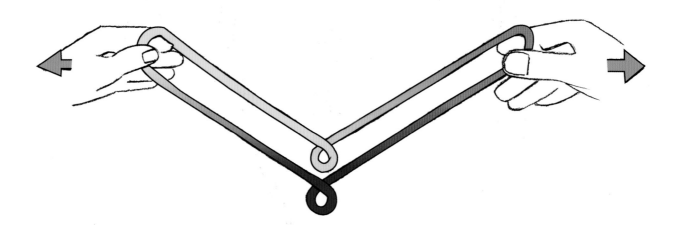

Waves

1. Hold loop loosely as the 'Calm sea.' Then turn one hand over (as if checking the time on your watch) sending 'Waves' to the other hand.

2. Temporarily release left hand as the 'Waves' arrive and they will 'Crash on the beach.'

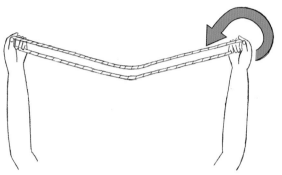

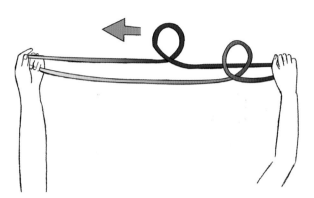

Bounce!

Hold the loop vertically, one hand above and lightly to one side of the other. Open fingers of top hand to release. If the other hand makes a sudden small upward movement the moment after the string reaches its lowest point the natural slight 'Bounce' is increased. Release as it reaches its highest point and the string continues its leap into the air! Catch it if you can!

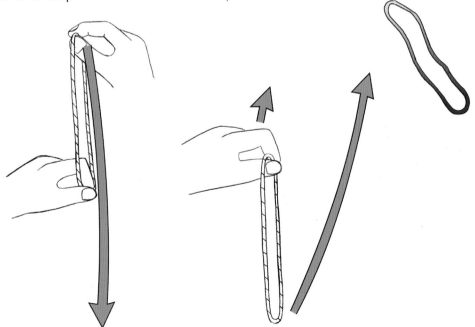

Serpent biting its own tail

Hold ends of loop with middle of loop hanging down. Move hands apart and lowest middle point starts to ascend. Make this movement fairly quickly (and diagonally upwards), releasing the hands as the middle reaches the horizontal. The momentum will send the loop higher and bring the ends together making the 'Serpent biting its own tail' in mid-air.

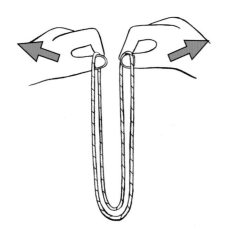
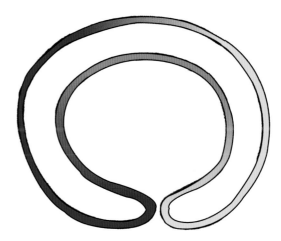

Handshake

1. Place trebled loop on wrist. Shake someone's hands saying, 'Pleased to meet you!'

2. Make the strings jump onto the other's hand, look surprised and ask 'How did you get that?'

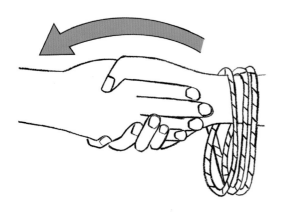
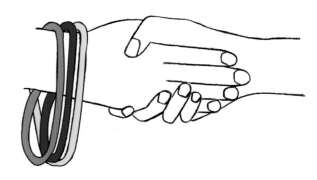

Spitting dragon

Hold 'Jumping Fish' (see page 21) between index fingers and middle fingers. Bend and then straighten fingers to make the 'Spitting dragon.' Note that when the fingers are bent the 'Necklace link' (see page 22) appears and when hands are held apart and feet are placed in the hanging loops it is possible to walk on 'Stilts.'

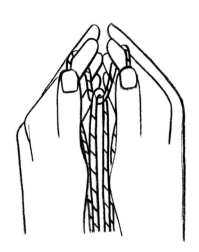 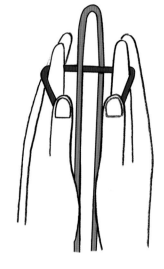

Wasp nest

The 'Wasp nest' comes from Queensland, Australia.

Smile!

The 'Smile' made with a doubled string becomes the 'Clown's Smile.'

 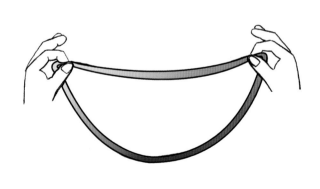

Stringing Stories Together

Figures woven together into longer stories. The name of the string figure (or the numbered stage in making the figure) is placed in brackets in the relevant part of the text.

The Dragon, the Princess and Jack

This is the story of the Dragon, the Princess and Jack. I'll just check the title in this Book: (page 127, 1&2) 'The Dragon, the Princess...' That's funny! Oh, I remember, the book opens from underneath too: 'and Jack.' (page 127, 3&4).

In a cave there lived a dragon. Whenever anyone approached it would spit fire! (Spitting dragon, page 131)

The dragon guarded a tall tower in which he had imprisoned a princess. She spent her days taking off and turning the rings on her fingers and admiring her necklace (Necklace link, page 22).

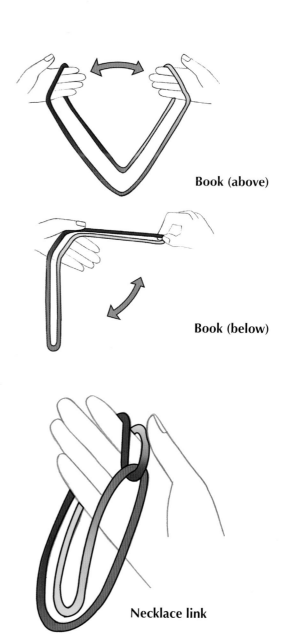

Book (above)

Book (below)

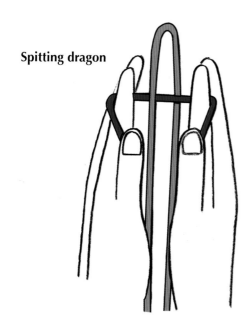

Spitting dragon

Necklace link

132

She had a small window through which she could see: The sun-in-the-sky, sun-in-the-sky, great and round, great and high! (Throw 'Balloons' figure (page 58) high on the word 'Sun').

She could also see the sea (Sea, page 129) and the waves crashing onto the beach (see Waves, page 129).

Balloon (representing sun)

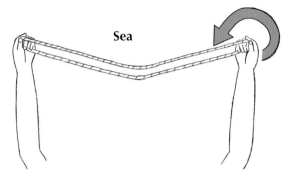

Sea

One day a storm cloud approached and she thought she saw people in the distance running for shelter. Suddenly there was a lightning flash (Lightning flash, page 88) and a thunder clap.

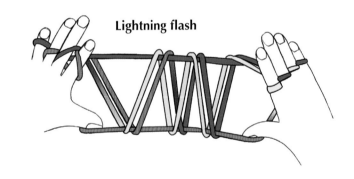

Lightning flash

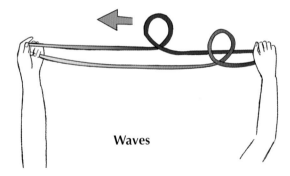

Waves

But the wind blew the storm away, the sea became calm again (Sea) and the storm disappeared the way dewdrops disappear in the early morning (Dewdrops, page 128).

Dewdrops

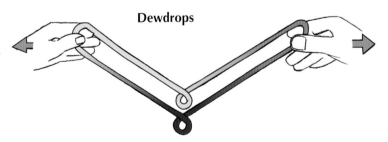

One Summer people started building a house: First they marked out the plot of land. (Start making Sealskin House, see page 52) They dug foundations (p.52, 1&2), built walls (p.52, 3), threw a tarpaulin over before the roof was made (p.52, 4). Two builders climbed inside to tie it down one windy night (p.53, 5). Then tilers climbed onto the roof to nail down tiles and make it waterproof (p.53, 6). Finally the house was built and was beautiful and strong (p.53, 7).

A family moved into the house. One day a boy ventured out and shot an arrow (Fish Spear, page 46) into a tree (hold vertically).

That night as he lay asleep (Man on a Bed, page 62) a figure spoke to him, 'Fetch your lost arrow and you will learn the secret of how to slay the dragon and save the princess.' (hold vertically for 'talking figure').

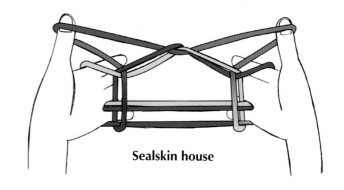

Sealskin house

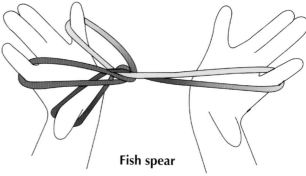

Fish spear

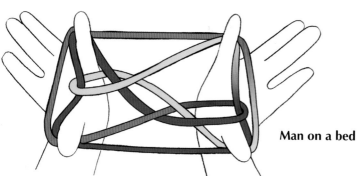

Man on a bed

He got up and went out into the night. He went past a waterfall where a fish was leaping (Bounce!, page 129). He caught the fish and then threw it back (Catch it!).

Bounce!

He approached the tallest tree, ducked under the lowest branch (Man Climbing a Tree, page 73, 1), got caught on some brambles, then lifted them off (p.73, 2), put his foot at the foot of the tree (p.73, 3) and started climbing: (p.73, 4) Up he climbed, one step at a time, one hand then the other, the wind blew, the leaves shivered. He stopped. He shivered. (Repeat 'climbing rhyme' until 'Man' reaches the top).

While he was looking for his arrow two mischievous gnomes approached, looked up, laughed and started sawing. (See 'Cradle to Sawing,' page 103 and 'Saw,' page 98, with a helper).

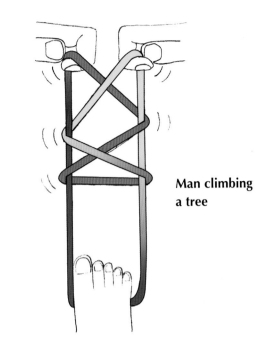

Man climbing a tree

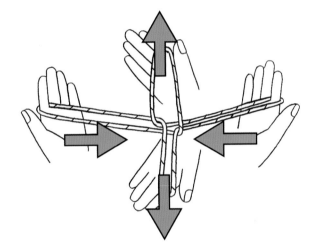

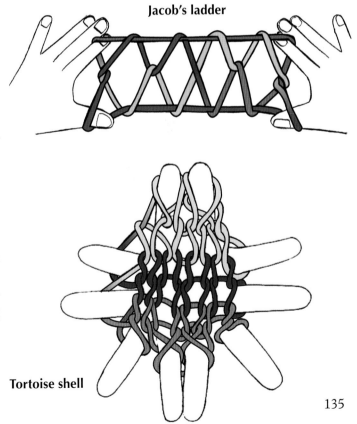

Jacob's ladder

The tree fell (Drop string and thank helper) and so did the young man. He had landed on moss. While on the ground a spider started weaving a web around him. As it wove it told him a secret and thanked him for throwing back the fish. (Make 'Jacob's Ladder' as a 'spider's web,' see page 38, or get someone in the audience to bring out a previously made 'Tortoise Shell,' page 104).

Tortoise shell

135

He woke up and knew what to do. He approached the dragon, went close to the dragon's left ear and shouted, "Boo!" The dragon leapt up and bit …its own tail! (Serpent biting its own Tail, page 130). It dropped dead, the princess was freed, they married and according to this book (page 127, 1&2) 'lived happily ever…' (Audience will remind you to open the 'Book' from below too) '…after!' (p. 127, 3&4)

Three Brothers find Treasure

Once the chief of a village wished to choose which of his three sons should have his treasures: his sword (Free or Caught, page 106, 3), his shield (p.107, 8) and everything he owned (Drop left little finger and right index to make figure dissolve). He took his box of treasure (Talking Mouth (2),

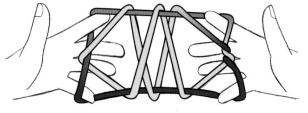

Free or Caught

page 77, 4), locked it (p.77, 5) and called his sons saying, (here the Talking mouth speaks becoming small with words like 'choose' and wide for words like 'go.' Talking Mouth (1) page 76) 'Go, seek adventure and after one year I will choose which of you shall have my treasures.' So off they went. And this story is about what they did and who, in the end, gets the treasures.

Serpent biting its own tail

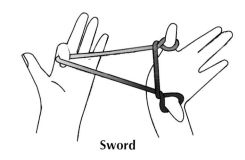

Sword

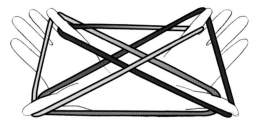

Talking mouth (2)

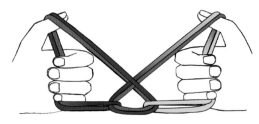

Talking mouth (1)

The first brother went round the back (Running Caribou, page 74, 1–3) and tied a rope (p.74, 4) around the neck (p.74f, 5–9) of his camel (Caribou). 'Come on, let's go!'

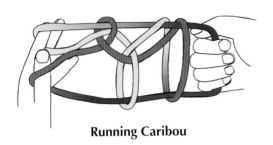

Running Caribou

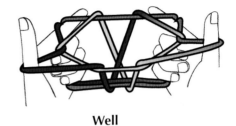

Well

They went until they came to a well (Sunflower, page 82, 4). After drinking he dipped his hands in the water and some drips fell on some flowers which immediately grew! (p.85, 16) He then noticed he was being watched by a farmer. They bowed to each other. (p.85, 17) 'So you've discovered my water. Come and see the rest of my farm.'

The farmer showed the barn (Frog, page 67, 2), water trough (page 67, 5) and a pig (Pig, page 72). 'I've so much to do on my farm,' the farmer said, 'Will you help me?' 'Yes!,' he replied and so stayed a year as a farmer.

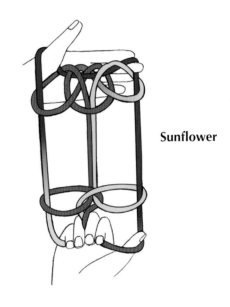

Sunflower

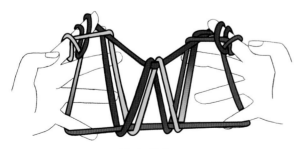

Little fishes

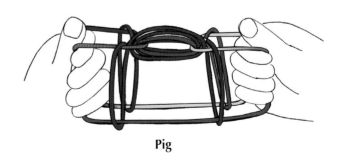

Pig

The second saw a Rabbit (page 90) running. 'I'll go that way.' He went towards the sea. There he met the harbour cat (Two Fish, page 80, 4) who was watching fishermen mending their nets.

One of them pointed at a boat with two masts (page 81, 8). 'Can you help me catch fish. There are just too many!' They went out to sea. Fish were swimming on both sides (page 81, 10) And he decided to stay a year as a fisherman.

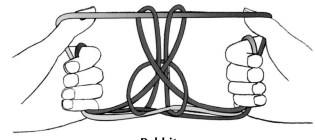

Rabbit

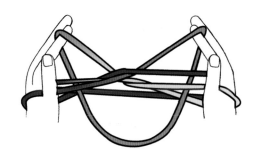

Cat's face

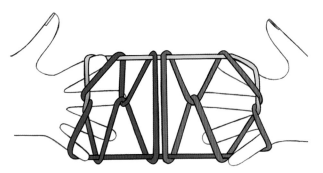

Two fish swimming away

The third did not know which way to go and so hid in a hollow tree waiting for inspiration (Porcupine, page 97, 6 — held vertically. 'I'll follow the first animal I see' An anteater scurried past him (Porcupine, page 96f) and ran through the open door of his house. 'So that's the way. Into my own house!'

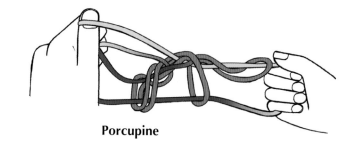

Porcupine

He chased it around the table and then the chair (Mosquito, page 45, 1). Then he noticed it licking up all the ants that were heading for the honey!

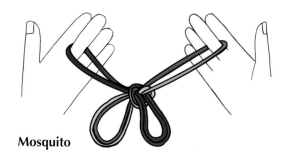

Mosquito

'What's worse, too many ants in the house or an anteater as a pet?' Just then a really unwelcome guest appeared. A huge fly! (Mosquito) It settled on one shoulder, then the other, his head, then his nose. He blew it away and it was gone. "I'm staying! I'm not going anywhere!" he declared.

The year was up and the three sons appeared in front of their father who asked (Talking mouth, page 76f) what they had done, 'And how much do you want my sword, my shield, my house and everything I own?' 'Your house?' 'I want to live on the farm,' said the first. 'I want to live by the sea,' said the second. So the treasures went to the third. "Now I'll open the treasure chest.' (Big Star, page 35, 9) He lifted out a string and pulled out a … (Big Star, page 34f) (Let the audience decide what it is.)

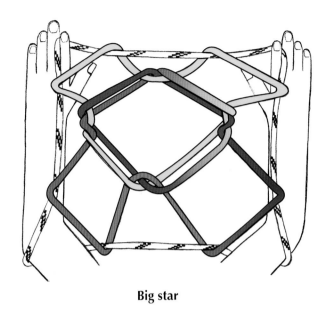

Big star

Ideas for Making Stories

Single Figure Stories

Choose a figure and use it to illustrate a factual account about the object or tell a story about it. You may wish to look at intervening shapes to see if they can be included. You can also use the quality of the movement ('somersaulting. digging, lifting' etc.) These words can be told while making the Five-Pointed Star (1), page 24. "One day Peter (right index) looked out of his window and saw his friend below. 'Come on up!' he called. His friend (left index) joined him for a cup of tea. They talked so long that the next time they looked out the stars were shining!'

Multiple Figure Stories

Choose a sequence and tell a story. The following story called 'One Day in Paris' goes with the 'Cup and saucer,' 'Eiffel Tower' sequence (see page 36f). 'Once a slim lady and another slim lady (index fingers take strings) sat down with two fat gentlemen (thumbs) for a cup of coffee. While they were drinking a woman with a witch's hat walked past. They followed her up the Eiffel Tower. When they got to the top only her scarf remained. Then even that disappeared. She must have been a witch!'

139

Sources

Simple Figures:

The Flag was shown to me by Davot Irving while he was a student of Philpots Manor School, Sussex, England.

Nibble Fish: Verse by Milly Reynolds.

Stars:

Half-Second Star: Bob Grimes.

Five-Pointed Star (1): My son Raphael added the Man by twisting the figure.

Five-Pointed Star (2): Navajo.

Navajo Star: Navajo.

Pole Star: Native American.

Elastic Band Star: Philippines.

Star in a Star: Philippines.

Five Person Star: Original.

Big Star: Navajo.

Crossed-Hands Star: Original.

Popular Figures:

Cup and Saucer: widespread (In New Caledonia it is a 'Canoe with Outrigger Attached to One Side,' in Japan it is a 'House' when held upside down and a 'Saki Cup' when right side up)

Jacob's Ladder is widespread (called 'Fishnet' and 'Osage Diamonds' in America, a 'Calabash Net for Carrying a Gourd' in Africa and in Quebec 'Le pont de Quebec' or 'Quebec Bridge')

Apache Door: Native American.

Parachute: Scotland (and elsewhere)

The Flying Bird (or Flying Parrot): Guyana, South America.

The Mosquito: widespread (the Fly in the Solomon Islands, a locust and even a Flying Fox elsewhere)

Fish Spear: widespread (a Fish spear or Harpoon in the Torres Straits, a duck spear in Alaska, and a coconut palm tree in Africa).

Stories:

The Owl or *Blinking Eye* comes from (among other places) the Hawaiian Island of Kauai. The story is by Jaimen McMillan.

Unravelling (Lal Ruanga Se Pal Ram) printed with some changes, was gathered by Alex Johnston Abraham in 1943 and published in *The Bulletin of the International String Figures Association,* Vol. 6, 133-144, 1999.

The Sealskin House is more normally known as *The Siberian House* from Big Diomede Island. The story is by Milly Reynolds.

The Straw House or *Grass Hut* comes from Africa. The story is by Milly Reynolds.

The Disappearing Mouse is a widespread trick.

Birthday Party is an original story (the 'Accordion' is known as 'Mrs Crab' in the South Sea Islands and as 'Elastics' in Japan)

Man on a Bed is from the Torres Straits.

3D Figures:

Eiffel Tower on Four Feet: France.

The Drum: Navajo.

The Tepee: Native American.

Navajo Butterfly: Navajo.

The Frog: The Guianas, South America.

The Pig: New Caledonia (the intervening 'W' shaped figure is 'Little Fishes' in the Torres Straits and in Africa 'Divining Bones' and the 'Winding of the Snake')

The Bird's Nest: Navajo.

The Racing Car: an original continuation.

Moving Figures:
Running Caribou: Inuit.
Man Climbing Tree: Australia.
Talking Mouth: Inuit.
The Bat: The Guianas, South America.
Two Fish: Caroline Islands.
Sunflower: a variation of the Well from the Torres Straits.

Other Figures:
Japanese Butterfly: Japan.
Ringing Bell: original continuation.
Lightning: Navajo.
The Rabbit: Native American.
Olympic Flag: Ronald Read, Canada.
The Porcupine: Native American.
Old Fashioned Telephone: original.

Partner Games:
Sawing: widespread.
Cutting the Hand: widespread.
Cat's-Cradle: widespread ('Candles' in UK is 'Chopsticks' in Korea, 'Mirror' in Denmark and 'River' in Japan.
'Soldier's Bed' or 'Church Window' in UK is 'Chessboard' in Korea and 'Fish pond' in America.
'Cat's Eye' in UK is 'Cow's Eye' in Korea and 'Horse's Eye' in Japan.
'Fish on the Dish' or 'Pig in the Pegs' in UK is a 'Musical Instrument' in Japan)
A Tortoise Shell: weaving on two hands is widespread.

Tricks:
The Lizard: Hawaii.
Wandering Loop: Japan.
Thumb Jump: original.
Through Thumb: widespread (similar to the Burmese Slip Trick) taught to me by Constantino Giorgetti.
One Hand Knot: unknown.
Smith's Secret: world-wide, (the trick my father showed me!)
Thrown Knot: Taught to me by Uzi Pinkerfeld.
Free or Caught: Caroline Islands.
Indian Rope Trick: widespread magic trick.
St. Lawrence Knot Trick: collected by David Titus from a Yupik Eskimo fisherman of Savoonga, St Lawrence Island, Alaska in 1999 and published in March 2000 *String Figure Magazine* with one different string crossing.
Cutting the Body: widespread.

String Things:
Monkey Chain: widespread. Scoubidou: Raphael Taylor.
Scoubidou Man: original.
Wrist Watch: Raphael Taylor.
Bolivian Footprint: Bolivia.
Whizzer: a widespread game.

Children's Inventions:
The Trampoline: Sandy Hagenbach.
Kite: Auren Lake Edwards. Camera: Danny Young.
Glove: Adam Blatchley.
Beard: Gareth Hilton.

Very Simple Figures:
Dewdrops, Waves, Bounce!, Serpent biting its own
    Tail, Spitting Dragon and Smile: original.
Wasp Nest: Australia.

Stringing Stories Together
'The Dragon, the Princess and Jack' and 'Three
    Brothers find Treasure': original stories.
Ideas For Making Stories: 'One Day in Paris' is based
    on a version used by Martin Baker.

Acknowledgments

Thank you Milly Reynolds and Jaimen McMillan
for use of rhymes and stories.
    Bob Grimes for the 'Half-Second Star.'
    Ronald Read of Canada for the 'Olympic Flag.'
    Teri West, storyteller, for inspiring the chapter
'Stringing Stories Together.'
    The International String Figure Association
(ISFA) for the story (printed with some changes)
from the Lushai Hills, gathered by Alex Johnston
Abraham in 1943 and published in *The Bulletin of
the International String Figures Association*, Vol. 6,
133-144, 1999.
    Hawthorn Press for use of selected text and
drawings from my previous string books *Pull the
Other One!* and *Now You See It …*
    Ann Swain for the Foreword.
    My wife, Claudine, and my son, Raphael, for
helping to invent, translate, teach, scan, enhance,
proofread and more.
    Lee Hannam for putting the images into the
correct format.
    Lori King for advising on corrections to the sec-
ond printing.

Contacts

Go to www.fingerstrings.co.uk for photos, videos
and strings.
    Email fingerstrings@me.com for further
information.

The International String Figure Association (ISFA)
The ISFA publishes a quarterly magazine, twice-
yearly newsletter and annual journal. For more
information write to:
ISFA Press, P.O. Box 5134, Pasadena, California
91117, USA
E-mail: webweavers@isfa.org
Website: www.isfa.org

Bibliography

Thank you ISFA for source material and the following books for ideas:

String Figures and How to Make Them Caroline
    Furness Jayne, Dover Books, 1906.
*The Story Vine: A Source Book of Unusual and
    Easy To Tell Stories from Around the World* Anne
    Pellowski, Macmillan, 1984.
Pull the Other One! Michael Taylor, Hawthorn Press,
    2000.
Now you see it … Michael Taylor. Hawthorn Press,
    2002.

Index